T0209716

MACAT

An Analysis of

# G. W. F. Hegel's

# Phenomenology of Spirit

Ian Jackson

ROUTLEDGE

Published by Macat International Ltd
24:13 Coda Centre, 189 Munster Road, London SW6 6AW.

Distributed exclusively by Routledge
2 Park Square, Milton Park, Abingdon, Oxon OX14 4RN
711 Third Avenue, New York, NY 10017, USA

*Routledge is an imprint of the Taylor & Francis Group, an informa business*

www.macat.com
info@macat.com

*Cataloguing in Publication Data*
A catalogue record for this book is available from the British Library.
Library of Congress Cataloguing-in-Publication Data is available upon request.
Cover illustration: Capucine Deslouis

ISBN 978-1-912302-99-4 (hardback)
ISBN 978-1-912127-18-4 (paperback)
ISBN 978-1-912281-87-9 (e-book)

**Notice**

# CONTENTS

# THE MACAT LIBRARY

The Macat Library is a series of unique academic explorations of seminal works in the humanities and social sciences – books and papers that have had a significant and widely recognised impact on their disciplines. It has been created to serve as much more than just a summary of what lies between the covers of a great book. It illuminates and explores the influences on, ideas of, and impact of that book. Our goal is to offer a learning resource that encourages critical thinking and fosters a better, deeper understanding of important ideas.

Each publication is divided into three Sections: Influences, Ideas, and Impact. Each Section has four Modules. These explore every important facet of the work, and the responses to it.

This Section-Module structure makes a Macat Library book easy to use, but it has another important feature. Because each Macat book is written to the same format, it is possible (and encouraged!) to cross-reference multiple Macat books along the same lines of inquiry or research. This allows the reader to open up interesting interdisciplinary pathways.

To further aid your reading, lists of glossary terms and people mentioned are included at the end of this book (these are indicated by an asterisk [*] throughout) – as well as a list of works cited.

Macat has worked with the University of Cambridge to identify the elements of critical thinking and understand the ways in which six different skills combine to enable effective thinking.
Three allow us to fully understand a problem; three more give us the tools to solve it. Together, these six skills make up the **PACIER** model of critical thinking. They are:

**ANALYSIS** – understanding how an argument is built
**EVALUATION** – exploring the strengths and weaknesses of an argument
**INTERPRETATION** – understanding issues of meaning

**CREATIVE THINKING** – coming up with new ideas and fresh connections
**PROBLEM-SOLVING** – producing strong solutions
**REASONING** – creating strong arguments

To find out more, visit **WWW.MACAT.COM.**

# CRITICAL THINKING AND *PHENOMENOLOGY OF SPIRIT*

## Primary critical thinking skill: REASONING
## Secondary critical thinking skill: CREATIVE THINKING

Hegel's 1807 *Phenomenology of Spirit* is renowned for being one of the most challenging and important books in Western philosophy. Above all, it is famous for laying out a new approach to reasoning and philosophical argument, an approach that has been credited with influencing Karl Marx, Jean-Paul Sartre, and many other key modern philosophers. That approach is the so-called "Hegelian dialectic" – an open-ended sequence of reasoning and argument in which contradictory concepts generate and are incorporated into a third, more sophisticated concept.

While the *Phenomenology* does not always clearly use this dialectical method – and it is famously one of the most difficult works of philosophy ever written – the Hegelian dialectic provides a perfect template for critical thinking reasoning skills. A hallmark of good reasoning in the construction of an argument, and the searching out of answers must necessarily consider contradictory viewpoints or evidence. For Hegel, contradiction is key: it is precisely what allows reasoning to progress. Only by incorporating and overcoming contradictions, according to his method, is it possible for thought to progress at all. While writing like Hegel might not be advisable, thinking like him can help take your reasoning to the next level.

## ABOUT THE AUTHOR OF THE ORIGINAL WORK

**Georg Wilhelm Friedrich Hegel** was born in Stuttgart, Germany, on August 27, 1770. In 1805 he became a professor at Jena University and began to write the first of his great philosophical texts there. A key figure in the explosion of philosophy in Germany at the turn of the nineteenth century, the sheer breadth of Hegel's thinking has influenced political philosophers for centuries. Closely associated with the University of Berlin in the latter part of his life, Hegel died from disease—possibly cholera—in 1831 at the age of 61.

## ABOUT THE AUTHOR OF THE ANALYSIS

**Ian Jackson** is a PhD student in the Politics, Philosophy and Religion department at Lancaster University. He is interested in the role new media plays in the dissemination of ideas.

## ABOUT MACAT

### GREAT WORKS FOR CRITICAL THINKING

Macat is focused on making the ideas of the world's great thinkers accessible and comprehensible to everybody, everywhere, in ways that promote the development of enhanced critical thinking skills.

It works with leading academics from the world's top universities to produce new analyses that focus on the ideas and the impact of the most influential works ever written across a wide variety of academic disciplines. Each of the works that sit at the heart of its growing library is an enduring example of great thinking. But by setting them in context – and looking at the influences that shaped their authors, as well as the responses they provoked – Macat encourages readers to look at these classics and game-changers with fresh eyes. Readers learn to think, engage and challenge their ideas, rather than simply accepting them.

'Macat offers an amazing first-of-its-kind tool for interdisciplinary learning and research. Its focus on works that transformed their disciplines and its rigorous approach, drawing on the world's leading experts and educational institutions, opens up a world-class education to anyone.'

**Andreas Schleicher**
**Director for Education and Skills, Organisation for Economic**
**Co-operation and Development**

'Macat is taking on some of the major challenges in university education ... They have drawn together a strong team of active academics who are producing teaching materials that are novel in the breadth of their approach.'

**Prof Lord Broers,**
**former Vice-Chancellor of the University of Cambridge**

'The Macat vision is exceptionally exciting. It focuses upon new modes of learning which analyse and explain seminal texts which have profoundly influenced world thinking and so social and economic development. It promotes the kind of critical thinking which is essential for any society and economy.
This is the learning of the future.'

**Rt Hon Charles Clarke, former UK Secretary of State for Education**

'The Macat analyses provide immediate access to the critical conversation surrounding the books that have shaped their respective discipline, which will make them an invaluable resource to all of those, students and teachers, working in the field.'

**Professor William Tronzo, University of California at San Diego**

# WAYS IN TO THE TEXT

## KEY POINTS

- G. W. F. Hegel was a German philosopher who was born in 1770. His text *Phenomenology of Spirit* was published in 1807.

- *Phenomenology of Spirit* explores the nature of human understanding; in it, Hegel was trying to define how we gain knowledge.

- Hegel not only broke with earlier philosophical traditions, he did so in a work that was very ambitious; *Phenomenology* tries to outline the whole of human experience.

### Who Was G. W. F. Hegel?

G. W. F. Hegel, the author of *Phenomenology of Spirit* (1807) was born in the German city of Stuttgart on August 27, 1770. At the age of three Hegel began his formal education. He studied at a gymnasium (a school with a reputation for being highly academic) from the age of six, then at the age of 18 went to the Tübinger Stift, a boarding school attached to the University of Tübinger. Although this school usually trained young men for entry into the Church, not all its students ended up following that career. Hegel left Tübinger in 1793 and found work as a tutor for an aristocratic family. He wrote several important essays during this period. In 1801 he moved to a city called Jena in Prussia—a country in what is today Northern Germany—where he became a lecturer at the university. By 1805 he had been promoted to the rank of "extraordinary professor" but he did not receive a salary, meaning that it became a financial necessity for him to finish *Phenomenology of Spirit*. In 1806 a battle took place at Jena between the French emperor Napoleon Bonaparte* and the Prussian* army. The town was almost destroyed and many university students fled. *Phenomenology* was published soon after.

By this time, Hegel had a reputation as an important thinker. *Phenomenology* was the starting point for all his later philosophical texts. It was an important step in the development of a philosophical field known as Idealism* (the idea that reality is made in the mind). Hegel's ideas were very complex, and there are still arguments as to their true meaning.

## What Does *Phenomenology of Spirit* Say?

*Phenomenology* is about how to approach the question "What really matters?" According to Hegel all reality is constructed by the mind although, crucially, the mind itself is not aware of it. Reality for Hegel is a vast, complex system that he called the Absolute.* According to Idealism, reality is not made up of the things that exist outside our heads; it is actually *within* the mind. But how can we begin to understand something so complex? Hegel's Absolute changed over time. He argued that only by understanding the Absolute in its entirety could we arrive at truth; understanding only part of it could logically only be partly true. Yet even partial truths were worth exploring, he believed; each part must contain a glimmer of truth. By carefully exploring it we might get closer to an understanding.

Imagine that a patient who cannot remember anything he has ever learned has just been given an orange that has been sliced into 16 segments. He has no memory of oranges at all. He is now told to examine the objects one at a time. After examining the first segment he might conclude that oranges are in fact small, wedge-shaped objects. As he explores further he might then realize his earlier theory was wrong, since the objects seem to fit together. The patient now moves through stages of thinking "an orange is wedge-shaped," "an orange is a semisphere," and so on. Each step provides more information about what an orange actually is. The curved shape of the first segment still *suggests* that the orange might be round even before it has been fully reassembled.

*Phenomenology*, however, is as much about the methodology of discovery—that is, the way discoveries are made—as it is about coming to conclusions. We can easily imagine the patient working out the nature of an orange by using his senses. Understanding the idea of the Absolute is more difficult. Hegel felt we needed a new way of looking at objects. Questions surrounding the nature of objects are part of a branch of philosophy known as ontology* that dates back to the ancient Greek philosopher Aristotle.* *Phenomenology* examines two important elements of this field: categories* and truth. Categories can be thought of as a way of separating objects from one another. Aristotle, for instance, created categories such as "substance," "quality," and "place." Without categories, Hegel argued, we can say nothing about what there *is*. Hegel's second concept of ontology tells us which things are "true" or "real." For Hegel, not everything was *equally* real. Chairs and numbers both exist, for example, but one is more "real" than the other.

Ideas like this were dominating German thought at the time. The philosopher Immanuel Kant's* *Critique of Pure Reason** (1781) had started an explosion of philosophical activity in Germany. Several different views were then developed. The author and philosopher F. H. Jacobi* tried to base knowledge on ethics, faith, and feeling. The poet and philosopher Friedrich Schlegel* and the writer Novalis* emphasized the intrinsic value of nature.* The philosophers K. L. Reinhold* and Johann Gottlieb Fichte* tried to add depth to Kant's

theories. Hegel and his friend Friedrich Wilhelm Joseph Schelling*
both put forward a more systematic explanation. Hegel assumed that his
readers would have a good understanding of Western philosophy, and
especially recent developments in the field. Because of this assumption,
however, *Phenomenology* can be difficult for a modern reader.

### Why Does *Phenomenology of Spirit* Matter?

*Phenomenology* is important because of its position in the history
of philosophy. The text is seen as Hegel's masterpiece, and it marks
the end of the period of German idealist philosophy that began
with Kant's *Critique of Pure Reason* (1781). This intense period of
intellectual thought is almost unique. Only Athens in the fifth century
B.C.E. and the European Renaissance*—the period following the
Middle Ages when European thinkers and artists turned to ancient
Greek and Roman models to reinvigorate European culture—can
match it. Even within this extraordinary period, *Phenomenology*
stands out as one of its most important texts.

The text can also be seen as the point at which philosophy's
boundaries with other disciplines began to blur. Although sociology
(the study of the nature and structure of society), history, economics,
and anthropology (the study of human cultures) did not develop
until years later, all were influenced by this text. Even on its own,
*Phenomenology* is one of the key texts of the nineteenth century.
Many of Hegel's core ideas, such as those on alienation* (at its core,
the process whereby individuals begin to see the world around
them as alien) and recognition,* are still debated today. For most
of the twentieth century, *Phenomenology* was seen from a Marxist
viewpoint—that is, it was understood, particularly in the Soviet
Union,* according to the analysis of society proposed in the work
of the economist and social theorist Karl Marx.* Paradoxically, the
collapse of the Soviet Union and the decline of Marxism* appears
to have reinvigorated interest in Hegel's idea. He has regained the

attention of leading scholars such as the American social theorist Francis Fukuyama,* for example. It is not just the variety of topics in *Phenomenology* that makes it so important: the text succeeds in shaping them into a single philosophical vision.

Since Hegel, no scholar has tried to write anything so ambitious as *Phenomenology*. Hegel's account of the history of Western consciousness* was a massive task but it was also only half the picture. He also tried to include an analysis of philosophical and cultural movements and the way they connected to one other. The text explored ideas that were quite different from earlier philosophy. Unlike much of Hegel's work, these ideas in their raw form are easy to understand. Hegel's argument was that philosophical truths emerged as history progressed, that the two developed side by side. Hegel's ideas had a profound impact on the course of history. Understanding the importance of such historicism* (the role of history on society) can do much to help students of any field understand historical events after 1806.

# SECTION 1
## INFLUENCES

# MODULE 1
## THE AUTHOR AND THE HISTORICAL CONTEXT

**KEY POINTS**

- Hegel's *Phenomenology* is a work of great importance that has influenced philosophy ever since it was published.

- Hegel's friendship with the philosopher Friedrich Wilhelm Joseph Schelling,* whom he met as a student, was important to his later role as lecturer at Jena University.

- Hegel wrote *Phenomenology* during the Napoleonic* wars (the conflicts provoked by the military actions of the French emperor Napoleon) in a period when the ideas of the German philosopher Immanuel Kant* were being revisited.

### Why Read This Text?

G. W. F. Hegel's *Phenomenology of Spirit* (German title: *Phänomenologie des Geistes*) is a unique work in Western philosophy in terms of its style, aims, and scope. Although it has been in and out of fashion since its publication in 1807, it is still one of the most influential works of the past two centuries. It consists of a long "Preface," a short methodological "Introduction," (that is, an introduction in which Hegel lays out the philosophical approach he will be using) and then eight chapters that chart the development of what Hegel calls consciousness.* It should be noted that Hegel's view of consciousness differs from what is commonly understood by the word.

The philosopher Immanuel Kant believed that there was a bridge between mind and matter. He argued that as you observe something through your senses it is understood, or interpreted,

> " An idea is always a generalization, and generalization is a property of thinking. To generalize means to think. "
>
> G. W. F. Hegel, *Elements of the Philosophy of Right*

through concepts.* In this way, someone suffering from amnesia, with no memory of ever having seen an orange, would not be so confused as you might expect when finally seeing one for the "first" time. Hegel, too, saw these concepts as "rules" that allow us to work out the properties of an object we see; the most general of these concepts form part of the categories* Hegel identified.

Hegel also argued that the individual consciousness tries to find self-knowledge through meeting other individual consciousnesses, so a collective consciousness builds up over time—an idea that is not as difficult to understand as it might seem. For example, a man who has lived his whole life in a desert can still understand what snow is by having it explained using concepts he is familiar with such as "white" and "cold." This idea of a collective consciousness is crucial to understanding Hegel. In fact, he developed it further by examining the collective consciousnesses of societies that he thought were crucial to the development of Western consciousness as a whole. These ideas had an enormous impact on the political evolution of the nineteenth and twentieth centuries.

It is perhaps because of the book's ambition and the variety of its themes that there are still arguments about the text. Scholars, such as the British professor of philosophy Stephen Houlgate,* have pointed out that the text is best understood as an introduction to Hegel's larger philosophical system.[1] Others, such as the French philosopher Jean Hyppolite,* believe that *Phenomenology* was a kind of *Bildungsroman*＊ (philosophical novel), telling the tale of the coming-of-age, education, and psychological growth of a character called "consciousness." This has led to the idea that Hegel was examining a process as it was actually unfolding.[2]

## Author's Life

Hegel was born in the city of Stuttgart, now in Germany but at that time in the Duchy of Württemberg, part of a number of affiliated central European territories known as the Holy Roman Empire.* Although Hegel's family was reasonably well off, several tragedies marked his early life. His mother died in September 1781 when he was 11 and the same fever that killed her almost took his life, too.[3]

He began his formal education at the age of three and proceeded to receive an excellent level of education. At the age of 18 he enrolled at a Protestant* seminary in Tübingen, Protestantism being one of the two largest branches of Christianity. Although seminaries were schools for those intending to become priests, not all students who studied there ended up serving the Church. Hegel and his friend, Friedrich Wilhelm Joseph Schelling,* for example, became philosophers.

Hegel began writing *Phenomenology* in 1805 at the University of Jena, where he had been an unpaid professor since 1801. The university was a famous philosophical center of excellence due to the work of both resident professor Johann Gottlieb Fichte* and Schelling. It was no coincidence that Hegel ended up in Jena; his connection to Schelling was key to his successful application to the institution.

## Author's Background

*Phenomenology* was completed during the chaos of Napoleon Bonaparte's* victory over the Prussian* army at the Battle of Jena* on October 14, 1806. Jena was a city in the state of Prussia, in what is today northern Germany. Having defeated Prussia, Napoleon began to demolish the Holy Roman Empire, the political landscape within which Hegel lived and worked. Fortunately, Hegel sent most of the manuscript to his publisher before he fled Jena with the final pages of *Phenomenology*, thereby ensuring its publication.

Hegel's unique perspective on these important international events added an extra element to an already groundbreaking work. But it was not just the shifting political landscape that was important; this was also an extremely fertile intellectual period.

The form and style of *Phenomenology* are strikingly original, but many of its central ideas were dominating German intellectual life at the time. The years following the publication of Immanuel Kant's *Critique of Pure Reason** in 1781 saw an explosion of philosophical activity in Germany. Among the positions that developed at this time were the novelist and philosopher F. H. Jacobi's* attempts to base knowledge on ethics* (concepts of right and wrong), faith, and feeling; the German Romanticism*—a movement in the arts that emphasized the importance of emotion as an aesthetic experience— of figures such as Friedrich Schlegel* and Novalis*; and the systematic adaptations of Kantianism*—the philosophy of Kant—proposed by the philosophers K. L. Reinhold* and Johann Gottlieb Fichte. Fichte's connection to the university where both Hegel and Schelling worked influenced the two men to follow his approach.

## NOTES

1   Stephen Houlgate, *The Opening of Hegel's Logic: From Being to Infinity* (West Lafayette, IN: Purdue University Press, 2006), 29–54.

2   Jean Hyppolite, *Genesis and Structure of Hegel's Phenomenology of Spirit*, trans. Samuel Cherniak and John Heckman (Evanston: Northwestern University Press, 1974).

3   Terry Pinkard, *Hegel: A Biography* (New York: Cambridge University Press, 2000), 3.

# ACADEMIC CONTEXT

## KEY POINTS

- G. W. F. Hegel was interested in whether or not the modern age had a distinctive character.
- Many German intellectuals were interested in classical Greek thought, especially that related to nature and values.
- Hegel was at the center of this intellectual world.

### The Work in its Context

To G. W. F. Hegel, the term "phenomenology"* had a very specific, complex meaning. Hegel was referring to what he described as a *scientific* treatment of the experience of an idealized consciousness.* We can think of this aspect of the work, perhaps, as a very sophisticated and rigorous thought experiment. As we have seen, Hegel's definition of consciousness is quite particular but so is his use of the term "scientific." It is important to note that the German word for science, *Wissenschaft*, is used for *any* systematic form of inquiry, not just the natural sciences. So, we should view Hegel's approach not as scientific but as *systematic*, a process with a beginning, middle, and end. Although Hegel expected his readers to understand this looser sense of the term, his move from normal modes of thought is still significant. Indeed, his idea to create a science out of consciousness's experience and his method for explaining its development were both highly original.

Hegel was a part of a larger community of German intellectuals who were all investigating various aspects of the modern world in which they lived. This diverse group had two things in common, aside from shared language and culture.

> **"** The spirit of a nation is reflected in its history, its religion, and the degree of its political freedom. The improvement of individual morality is a matter involving one's private religion, one's parents, one's personal efforts, and one's individual situation. The cultivation of the spirit of the people as a whole requires in addition the respective contributions of folk religion and political institutions. **"**
>
> G. W. F. Hegel, *On the Prospects for a Folk Religion*

First they had an almost obsessive interest in classical Greek\* culture inspired by the art historian Joachim Winkelmann's\* *The History of Ancient Art* (1764). German academics from Johann Wolfgang von Goethe\* and Johann Gottfried Herder\* to Friedrich Schiller,\* and even Hegel's contemporary Friedrich Schlegel,\* had been inspired by the idea that Greek art was the finest the world had ever seen. Nostalgia for the world of the Greek city-state, the *Polis*, was widespread. So was the belief that the modern world could never achieve either the same levels of beauty in art, or virtue in political character, as the Greeks. Hegel, however, differed. While he shared their popular love of Greece, he set out to combat nostalgia.

The second uniting principle was that the work of these intellectuals can be viewed either as a critical response to, or development of, Kant's\* so-called "critical" philosophy, a dominant idea of the 1780s and early 1790s.

### Overview of the Field

*Phenomenology of Spirit* deals with issues that were central to the intellectual life of the period. Hegel was working in a complicated field known as Idealism\* that had many subdivisions. One of the subdivisions was in direct opposition to Materialism.\* Immanuel Kant's view, known as

Transcendental Idealism,* states that the mind shapes the world around us into what we perceive as reality; whether reality is ultimately just in the mind was not something Kant committed to.

Hegel's view, known as Absolute Idealism, differs from Transcendental Idealism in a number of ways. Hegel insists that reality can only be understood as a whole, and introduces the idea of a collective consciousness. This argues against the idea that those around an individual tend to influence his or her views. Hegel also created the concept of a developmental history, according to which societies examine ways of thinking, reject them, and replace them with something more refined. Since these philosophical ideas had to do with the creation of political systems, they had a real-world relevance. The political climate was volatile, and German thinkers were now forced to take a stand on the question of political authority.

When Hegel wrote *Phenomenology,* he was aware of the need to have an independent voice in a world that was becoming dominated by ideologies. He had been viewed as a supporter of his colleague Friedrich Wilhelm Joseph Schelling's* so-called "identity philosophy,"* a philosophical approach concerned with things such as the permanence of personal identity but *Phenomenology* showed that Hegel had a legitimate voice of his own.[1] His departure from the Kantian school was a major development in the history of philosophy—and an opportunity for academic philosophy to engage with the political world.

### Academic Influences

Hegel was clearly influenced by the work of Kant, whose ideas about a universal "invisible church"*—invisible because it was internal and founded on pure reason—are easy to see in *Phenomenology*. It was a concept with practical and political implications. The "invisible church" provided philosophical reasons to oppose orthodoxy, hierarchy, and the patrician* politics (rule by a group of families) of the Holy Roman Empire,* a group of territories in central Europe.

Hegel believed that modernity (the modern era, often assumed to have begun in the late fifteenth century) was essentially different from the ancient world. Modernity possessed distinct values based upon individual freedom and modern citizens needed to appreciate the nature of these values and the reasons for their existence.

Although Hegel found Kant's emphasis on individual autonomy*—the power to make one's own decisions—an inspiring challenge to traditional authority, Hegel's ideas of collective consciousness somewhat diluted the power of that autonomy. Similarly, Hegel found Kant's supposed demolition of natural theology*—roughly, the attempt to find religious truths from the observation of the natural world—highly inspiring. The traditional rationalist* philosopher Moses Mendelssohn* (rationalism being a branch of philosophy founded on the idea that knowledge comes from reason) called Kant the "all-destroyer," and the young minds that followed Kant were eager to build on the foundations he had torn down. Indeed, by arguing that there was no rational proof for belief in God and the soul, Kant's work challenged the whole of traditional theology in fundamental ways.

Hegel, we know, came to the conclusion that the Absolute was in the end something that could be understood. During his time studying in Tübingen he had violently disagreed with his teacher, the theologian Gottlob Storr,* over Kant's idea that God and the soul were postulates of pure practical reason.* A "postulate" is a theoretical proposition intended to test an idea, so by this, Kant had meant that such things were noumenal* (a word he used to describe unknowable things, such as the afterlife) and therefore neither provable nor disprovable.

## NOTES

1    Terry Pinkard, *Hegel: A Biography* (Cambridge: Cambridge University Press, 2000), 221–30.

# THE PROBLEM

## KEY POINTS

- In the wake of Immanuel Kant's* theories, many thinkers moved into the field of ontology*—the study of the nature of being.

- Although Kant's ideas dominated thought in Germany, they were so complex that many different conclusions were reached.

- Hegel also adapted Kant but did so in a unique way. *Phenomenology* might have had no predecessors, but because of its complexity, it had no successors either.

### Core Question

The core question of G. W. F. Hegel's *Phenomenology of Spirit* is "what really matters?" While the language used to discuss the Absolute* (for Hegel, an unchanging, independent, and ultimately unknowable truth) may be unfamiliar, Hegel's interest in how objects *are* in fact belongs to the field of ontology, a field of inquiry that deals with the "doctrine of being."* He split his analysis into two parts that he named "conceptions".

The first conception tried to clarify the general concepts or categories* that can be used to decide what "exists." The Greek philosopher Aristotle* believed that there were 10 categories; everything that existed fitted into one of them. For example, you might encounter an object and declare that it fitted into the category "substance." For Kant this was simply a matter of judgment. For Hegel, however, *analyzing* these categories was essential. It is possible to think about the categories using simpler terms than those that Hegel

> 66 Knowledge of the Idea of the absolute ethical order depends entirely on the establishment of perfect adequacy between intuition and concept, because the Idea itself is nothing other than the identity of the two. But if this identity is to be actually known, it must be thought as a made adequacy. 99
>
> G. W. F. Hegel, *System of Ethical Life*

or Kant provided. How can one understand a hot cup of tea? The categories of "hot," "wet," and "drink" tell us something. But these categories themselves also fit into more general categories: "drink," for example, fits into the category "liquid."

The second conception tells us which things have the status of being truly real. This is asking a very simple question. Is everything about which we can have precise thoughts using categories equally real? This returns us to the earlier question: is a chair more real than an abstract concept such as a number? Hegel's *Phenomenology* tackled this in a very specific and original way: the first concept of ontology clarified the question of *how things are*, while the second clarified the question of *what there is*.

### The Participants

In many respects, G.W. F. Hegel's *Phenomenology of Spirit* is unique. In terms of its central claims, method, and style, and the combining of its wide and distinctive range of topics, it has no real predecessors or successors. This does not mean, however, that later philosophers did not try to develop its ideas or that its themes did not attract interest at the time.

For example, Hegel's famous discussion in *Phenomenology* of the master-slave dialectic\* (a struggle between two consciousnesses, one seeking to be recognized as superior, the other not giving that recognition) had implications for a wide range of philosophical topics. Although mainly a contribution to modern theories of natural rights* (rights possessed by all, regardless of social or moral codes), his theory would have been seen by readers in relation to the philosopher Johann Gottlieb Fichte's* analysis of the same issue of master and slave. Indeed, it was Fichte who introduced the idea of mutual recognition* (the part of us that wants to be recognized as a human being) to describe the basic freedoms to which rational beings are entitled and provide a justification for those freedoms.

The English political philosopher Thomas Hobbes* had argued that beings with their own motivations and desires end up in conflict with each other and must make a social contract* to have long-term relations.[1] The political philosopher John Locke,* meanwhile, followed by looking at the *nature* of the individual self-consciousness to find rules of social behavior approved by God. He concluded that "personal identity is a matter of psychological continuity."[2] The French philosopher René Descartes* came to a different conclusion, saying, "man innately knows basic logical propositions."[3] All of these questions basically asked "what makes me the person that I am?" For Descartes, the answer was the soul. But for Locke, the answer was more complex. He argued that an "empty mind" was shaped by experiences that came from sensations and reflections.[4] Locke's views on consciousness predated Kant.

Fichte, however, was able to draw on Kantian* arguments that explained the *conditions* of self-consciousness that Descartes and Locke took for granted. He *identified* those conditions with the kind of conflict theorized by Hobbes. In other words, the existence of human conflict is due to our sense of self. Although this manages to describe the origin of conflict, it does not explain conflict's basic nature. This can be thought of as the "grudge" that our sense of identity has with the rest of the world. For Fichte the answer had to do with recognition; we reach the status of rational, rights-bearing, free beings when one consciousness recognizes another consciousness.

## The Contemporary Debate

*Phenomenology* is often seen as the key text in which Hegel explores the idea that philosophical truth is basically developmental, and that it emerges as history progresses. This is an idea that differs from previous philosophy, but Hegel was working in a philosophical tradition. The influence of Immanuel Kant is clear in Hegel's attempt to take Kant's ideas on transcendental idealism* one step further. Hegel's influences stretch back as far as the ancient Greek philosopher Plato* and included both René Descartes and the Dutch thinker Benedictus de Spinoza.* The debate at the time, however, was dominated by those thinkers who were also trying to modify or complete the works of Kant.

The main reason for this interest in the Absolute was Kant's discussion of the "unconditioned" in the section of his *Critique of Pure Reason*\* entitled the "Transcendental Dialectic."\* There, Kant discussed absolute objects: objects that establish our empirical* knowledge (that is, our knowledge drawn from experience) and that do not themselves require grounding. Indeed the term "absolute" was common in post-Kantian Idealist philosophy. Fichte placed the "absolute I" or "ego" at the center of his philosophy. Schelling's* philosophy of the absolute was itself an attempt to combine Fichte's "absolute I" with Spinoza's pantheistic* (the belief that God and nature are one) and supposedly "absolute" view of nature.

## NOTES

1 Thomas Hobbes, *Leviathan: Cambridge Texts in the History of Political Thought*, ed. Richard Tuck (Cambridge, UK; New York: Cambridge University Press, 1991).

2 Namita Nimbalkar, "John Locke on Personal Identity," *Mens Sana Monographs*. 9.1 (2011): 268.

3 Nimbalkar, "John Locke on Personal Identity," 268.

4 Nimbalkar, "John Locke on Personal Identity," 268.

# THE AUTHOR'S CONTRIBUTION

## KEY POINTS

- Hegel's aim in writing *Phenomenology of Spirit* was to provide an introduction to what he called "philosophical science."

- Hegel's primary contribution was to invent his own method for arriving at conclusions. He called this his "Science of Logic."

- Hegel tackled ideas that were common in the post-Kantian* world, such as the problem of working out what was real and the nature of mutual recognition.*

### Author's Aims

G. W. F. Hegel's principle aim in *Phenomenology of Spirit* was to discover "what really matters." He wanted to create a new way of tackling some of the concepts that had been introduced by the philosopher Immanuel Kant.* He argued that his "Science of Logic" was necessary if we were to have any hope of understanding the Absolute.*

By examining the text's influence on a case-by-case basis Hegel's aims will be clear. For example, Hegel's contribution to the master-slave dialectic* led him to disagree with Johann Gottlieb Fichte's* notion that mutual recognition simply dawned on beings as a rational fact. Hegel argued instead that the idea of recognition developed logically during conflict. Hegel supported his colleague Friedrich Wilhelm Joseph Schelling's* idea that we could understand the Absolute by using Kant's concept of "intellectual intuition."[1] He distanced himself from the idea that the Absolute had no structure

> 66 Hegel's theoretical philosophy ... can best be brought into focus by considering Hegel's relationship to Kant. In short, Kant famously holds that our knowledge is restricted: we can have no theoretical knowledge of things as they are 'in themselves.' All should agree that Hegel seeks to overturn this restriction, or to establish knowledge which is not limited in this way—to establish knowledge of 'what is truly in itself.' 99
>
> James Kreines, "Hegel's Metaphysics: Changing the Debate"

and that our understanding of it began immediately.[2] Hegel wanted to show that "intuition" and the gradual unfolding of a structure were one and the same.

For Hegel, the conflict itself was less important than the process, because it could be understood as a logical step in the development of an identity. Since Hegel had emphasized the importance of collective consciousness (roughly, an idea based on our shared desire for self-knowledge) it followed that human history, too, was a process dominated by the master-slave dialectic. Hegel's purpose was ambitious: he wanted to unravel the entire developmental history of Western civilization.

### Approach

From what Hegel termed philosophical science came the system of categories* that make up the Absolute. We should remember that Hegel's Absolute consists of what truly or ultimately exists and that it is contained within the mind. *Phenomenology*, as an introduction to that science, both surveys and evaluates a *series* of ontological* theories (that is, theories concerned with an inquiry into the nature of being). Its real importance though lies in its novel attempt to answer another traditional philosophical question, one that goes back to the seventeenth century and the French philosopher René Descartes.* We can think of this as the question: is ontology even possible? Or rather, is it even possible to know what is real?

Hegel's approach was novel because he addressed such doubts in a systematic way that he saw as a scientific exercise. *Phenomenology*, he noted, is a "self-completing skepticism."[3] Hegel was willing to challenge every possible skeptical doubt about how our minds might relate to what there is in truth, until there was nowhere left for the skeptic to go. At this point he believed we would end up not with empty skeptical doubt, but with real content. This content would be nothing other than knowledge of the Absolute, of what is *real*.

It may seem strange that a book that covers themes as diverse as the Roman conception of a person and eighteenth-century pseudoscience addresses only one central question. Yet Hegel is clear that his main subject is *whether* and *how* we can know the Absolute, how objects are in their "actuality" or "in truth."

## Contribution in Context

Hegel's desire in *Phenomenology of Spirit* to base philosophy on the Absolute would not have surprised his contemporaries, since the term was common in post-Kantian* Idealist* philosophy ("Idealism" being an approach founded on the idea that "reality" is constructed in the mind). Johann Gottlieb Fichte, for example, placed the "Absolute I" or "ego" at the center of his philosophy. Friedrich Wilhelm Joseph Schelling's philosophy of the Absolute was itself an attempt to combine Fichte's "Absolute I" with the Dutch philosopher Benedictus de Spinoza's* pantheistic* and supposedly "Absolute" view of nature. The main inspiration for the contemporary mania for the Absolute was, of course, not Hegel, but the passage of Immanuel Kant's *Critique of Pure Reason* titled "Transcendental Dialectic."*

However, since we can see Hegel's arguments as they developed in texts written while he was in Jena, we can trace his original contribution to the field. Surviving notes from his lectures, letters to friends, drafts of his early "logic," and his groundbreaking piece *Philosophy of Spirit* of 1804–5 provide direct evidence that Hegel had been developing techniques that he would later employ in *Phenomenology*.

Such drafts and sketches have given rise to a scholarly debate about a so-called "Ur-Phenomenology" (an earlier version of the book). Did Hegel originally intend to write a nonhistorical psychological proof or "deduction" of his version of the Absolute, adding in historical sections later? Among those scholars who think there was an "Ur-Phenomenology," there is also a dispute over which sections of the finished work correspond to it.[4] Whatever position one takes on this, the main philosophical issue is whether Hegel's historical and nonhistorical forms of argument stand in tension. The debate continues today.

Throughout his time in Jena, Hegel's study of thought and meaning, and indeed of philosophy's place within a historical setting, ultimately fed into *Phenomenology*. As a result, *Phenomenology* represents the point at which the epistemology* (the study of knowledge) and metaphysics* (the branch of philosophy that examines the nature of reality) of German Idealism*—and, many argue, of Western philosophy itself—takes a fundamental turn toward the acknowledgment of history.

## NOTES

1   James Kreines, "Hegel's Metaphysics: Changing the Debate," *Philosophy Compass* 1.5 (2006): 473.

2   G. W. F. Hegel, *Phenomenology of Spirit*, trans. A. V. Miller (Oxford: Oxford University Press, 1977), 72.

3   Hegel, *Phenomenology*, 78.

4   For an account of the various positions taken in this debate, see Michael N. Forster, *Hegel's Idea of a Phenomenology of Spirit* (Chicago: University of Chicago Press), Part 4.

# SECTION 2
## IDEAS

# MAIN IDEAS

## KEY POINTS

- Hegel wished to create a scientific method for establishing truth. He identified self-consciousness with a struggle for recognition* and pinpointed this struggle as part of an engine that drives history.

- Hegel wished to show that self-consciousness is essential to any understanding of an object.

- These main ideas are presented in the preface to the book. They are cryptic and hard to understand.

### Key Themes

The key themes of G. W. F. Hegel's *Phenomenology of Spirit* are first, the nature and limits of human knowledge, and second, his belief that the influential philosopher Immanuel Kant's work on Idealism* (an approach to philosophy founded on the idea that we construct "reality" in our minds) had not provided the necessary tools Kant needed to achieve his objective. His subject was the entire developmental history of Western civilization including its history, culture, morality, religion, perception, consciousness, and knowledge. In order to understand this, Hegel's main theme needs to be separated into four categories*: thought and meaning depend on the community; access to objects as they are "in truth" is always mediated by concepts; thought and being are identical; history is the progressive education of human beings toward freedom.

Hegel was aware that his project would require a thorough understanding of the nature of the Absolute* (and crucially how

> **❝** Our epoch is a birth–time, and a period of transition. The spirit of man has broken with the old order of things hitherto prevailing, and with the old ways of thinking, and is in the mind to let them all sink into the depths of the past and to set about its own transformation. **❞**
>
> G. W. F. Hegel, *Phenomenology of Spirit*

his view of it differed from other philosophers'.) He therefore begins by showing how an individual consciousness's relation to an object requires increasingly complex conceptual frameworks until it understands that self-consciousness is essential to its knowledge. What is more, he shows that our struggle for mutual recognition is not just basic to human knowledge. It also drives the process of "reevaluating" the conceptual framework in the first place.

### Exploring the Ideas

It is possible to gain a sound understanding of *Phenomenology* by bearing in mind the text's four central ideas:

1. Thought and meaning are essentially dependent upon the community.
2. Thought's access to objects as they are "in truth" is always mediated by concepts.
3. Thought and being are identical.
4. History is the progressive education of human beings toward freedom.

Our reason is not given to us as a "rulebook" that tells us how we should interact with the world. Hegel argues that it does not come from intuition or a process of reasonable contemplation (ratiocination).* Instead, it is created by the internal history of our attempts over time to make sense of the world.

As an example, consider a baby attempting to understand what an orange is. Putting it in its mouth, the baby discovers first that the orange is too big and second that it is not very tasty. The fact that the flesh of the orange actually *is* tasty, is knowledge that is not available to the baby. This orange represents one of Hegel's "things with many properties," and so needs to be understood by way of his two conceptions.[1] This requires the education of consciousness, a process of overcoming errors, without which progress cannot be made. Here we again encounter the master-slave dialectic,* along with Hegel's insistence that "self-consciousness exists in and for itself when, and by the fact that, it so exists for another."[2]

Self-consciousness is created by an encounter between two beings who only realize they are self-conscious because of the encounter itself. A fight to the death will lead to what Hegel described as an "abstract negation" (failure of the process): the victor claims lordship over the defeated who, being dead, cannot recognize the master. Only if one of the two is unafraid of death can he achieve mastery. The slave now has to make things for his master. In the end he begins to see himself in those products and achieves an independent self-consciousness. The master, who now depends on the things the slave has made, has become as much a slave as the slave himself.

Progress is only achieved when the master-slave relationship has been reduced. This can be understood in a simple way by looking at history as a process of stages. Greece, as a slave state, gave way to the less restrictive system of serfdom.* This was, in turn, replaced by the citizenship of liberal democracies in which individual freedom was protected. In each case, more freedom is allotted to the "slave" and the master becomes less reliant on the slave's products.

### Language and Expression

Hegel that knew his philosophical language was challenging—full of technical and unfamiliar vocabulary—but he felt that it was needed. He believed that concepts changed their meaning in different environments. *Phenomenology* drives home this lesson, repeating the same terms throughout the work, yet subtly shifting their meanings as they appear in different contexts.

While the work may appear to be an awkward attempt to glue together psychology and epistemology* (the study of knowledge) on the one hand, and history and epistemology on the other, both these aspects combine to produce an all-encompassing vision. The key to understanding this is to recognize how the idea of holism* (the conception that all parts of a system must be understood as a whole) unites Hegel's key ideas about grasping both the structure of reality and the structure of social units. The Absolute can be understood only by seeing how individual concepts produce further concepts and how they gain their meaning through their relation to those new concepts. This should be seen as a process but not a method; it can be revealed only in practice as it is applied to any given situation. This is the essence of dialectical* thinking.

When Hegel introduces the ideas of "negation" and "mediation," he is referring to concepts producing new concepts. These two new terms refer to the complex process required to create the new concept (the negation) and its relationship to the old concept (the mediation). This is a three-stage process that was later described as a triadic structure* of thesis (a thought that has proved to be unsatisfactory), antithesis (an idea that confirms our suspicion about the flaws in the thesis, but which is itself flawed) and, finally, synthesis (a new thought, which will itself be challenged). In this structure, an unstable concept first gives way to another concept. The notion that an individual can only enter into successful relations with another if the second person, too, stands in negative and mediated relations also forms the basis of Hegel's theories of mutual recognition. Many of the topics of *Phenomenology* are about elaborating the holistic structure shared between individuals who recognize each other, and the reality of which they are a part.

## NOTES

1   G. W. F. Hegel, *Phenomenology of Spirit,* trans. A. V. Miller (Oxford: Oxford University Press, 1977), 67

2   Hegel, *Phenomenology,* 111.

# MODULE 6
# SECONDARY IDEAS

## KEY POINTS

- Hegel's views on mutual recognition* came from his analysis of the master-slave dialectic.* His views on holism* (the idea that parts of a system must be understood in terms of their relation to the whole) gave way to concepts of a divine-human identity in which our consciousness and God were merged into a single thing.

- Hegel's theories on mutual recognition altered the course of human history. The idea of a divine-human identity took theology in new directions and placed value on the importance of humanity in the concept of God.

- The influence of the idea of mutual recognition cannot be understated. Although students require a good understanding of history to appreciate its impact fully, major events such as the Russian Revolution* of 1917 and even entire periods such as the Cold War* can be traced back to Hegel's thinking.

### Other Ideas

The secondary themes of G. W. F. Hegel's *Phenomenology of Spirit* include his ideas of holism and dialectical* thinking. Hegel's theory of holism, although deeply controversial, says that concepts can only be understood in terms of their relation to the whole. In short, to understand what really matters, the whole must be understood first.

In *Phenomenology*, such ideas are most apparent in parts of the text that examine theology, the systematic study of scripture. This can be seen in the "Religion" section and its transition into "Absolute Knowledge." From there, the ideas of divine–human identity are

> **❝** It was [Karl] Marx who had first discovered the great law of motion of history, the law according to which all historical struggles, whether they proceed in the political, religious, philosophical or some other ideological domain, are in fact only the more or less clear expression of struggles of social classes, and that the existence and thereby the collisions, too, between these classes are in turn conditioned by the degree of development of their economic position, by the mode of their production and of their exchange determined by it. This law ... has the same significance for history as the law of the transformation of energy has for natural science. **❞**
>
> Friedrich Engels, Preface to third German edition of Karl Marx's *The Eighteenth Brumaire of Louis Bonaparte*

most accessible. Having understood that every stage of any given process is partial and potentially untrue, it becomes clear that a new way of thinking is needed: the dialectic. For Hegel, totality contains within itself the partial truths of prior stages that it has overcome. Dialectical thought, then, is a process; it is more than a means simply to come to a conclusion.

The importance of dialectics cannot be understated, especially its impact on history. The political theorist Karl Marx,* for example, was deeply influenced by Hegel's ideas and eventually added the idea of mutual recognition to his wider theories on class struggle,* which, he theorized, would end when working people organized themselves to end their exploitation at the hands of the ruling and the business classes. This had a deep impact on the course of history. The influence of Hegel's idea of alienation* (that is, the result of failures in mutual recognition) was not limited to its obvious connection to Marxism-Leninism,* the founding ideology of the Soviet Union.* Instead, it is important to realize that it has affected a wide range of academic fields and social and political movements for more than 150 years.

## Exploring the Ideas

Dialectical thinking can be explained in terms of an automobile engine that has been spread out in parts across the ground. To understand the engine properly, one must assemble it. Each piece, when placed in the right order, gives us a partial truth about the nature of the engine and its function. Even placing it in the wrong order reveals some truth because knowledge of its incorrect position is still useful.

Once fully constructed, the engine has achieved totality—and yet it still contains all of the earlier partial truths. Critically, nothing has been lost. Hegel likened this to a spiral. Think of a wheel with a mark on it where it touches the ground. When the wheel is rolled 360 degrees, it is clear that although the mark is still touching the ground, it has moved from its original position.

This process is complete within separate categories,* which for Hegel were: being, becoming, one, many, essence, existence, cause, effect, universal, mechanism, and "life." As each process is examined and revealed to be only a partial truth, it in turn creates another category that shows more promise. This rejection of one category toward another more "refined" category is known as *negation*.

The idea can easily be applied to mutual recognition. The state of mutual recognition, Hegel suggests, does not occur spontaneously between human beings. Instead, individuals must overcome social relations in which they do not recognize one another as equal authorities on truth and ethics. True self-knowledge, social stability, and a legitimate political order depend upon mutual recognition. But they result from a process in which recognition is not matched: "At first, it [the "process of recognition"] will exhibit the side of the inequality of the two, or the splitting-up of the middle term into the extremes which, as extremes, are opposed to one another, one being only *recognized*, the other only *recognizing*."[1] Mutual recognition in this sense is just the accepting and respecting of another being.

Such recognition remains fundamental to human psychology; the desire for recognition is the desire for equality, as relevant to class struggle as it is to feminism, the struggle against racial inequality (or apartheid)* or any other inequality. Throughout *Phenomenology*, Hegel shows different examples of the psychological and social harm he sees resulting from failures of recognition in different cultures and political systems. This is the harm he calls "alienation."

Meanwhile, the idea of divine-human identity saw Hegel drawing on Incarnation theology* (the study of the Incarnation*— the Virgin Birth and human life of Jesus Christ) and Benedictus de Spinoza's* pantheistic* vision—his equation of God and nature. Hegel certainly identified his idea of the Absolute* with God. As we have seen, Hegel's Absolute is neither a static thing nor a theoretical idea. It is instead the process of developing a system for understanding reality over historical time. Hegel's theory of divine-human identity, therefore, does not say that any given human or group is divine. He says we will find the divine in the human attempt to bring to consciousness a rational structure that includes the mind and the world.

### Overlooked

Since its publication, very little of *Phenomenology* has escaped analysis. This is particularly evident in the 1997 commentary on *Phenomenology* written by the British philosophy scholar H. S. Harris*, whose list of studies specifically related to Hegel's philosophy runs to 70 pages.[2] Ideas in the text have been applied to new problems that have arisen outside the area of philosophy. For example, the Hegel commentator and philosopher Michael Quante* has shown interest in the chapter subsection dealing with logical and psychological laws and with phrenology (the "science" of analyzing a person's character and potential from the bumps on their head) and physiognomy* (the "science" of reading a person's character from their face). At first sight it seems surprising that Hegel's mocking treatment of phrenology and physiognomy should receive such attention now but Hegel was arguing against understanding logical phenomena in terms of their physical states. Philosophers such as Quante find his arguments useful in critiquing reductionist* programs (that is, analytical methods based on a "reductive" over-simplification). They also provide useful clues for philosophers working in modern action theory,*[3] which discusses the causes and significance of human actions.

An examination of the historical reconstruction and dialectical development of *Phenomenology* might also assist in other problematic areas of political and moral philosophy. Much contemporary discussion about ethical and political value consists in battles between "realist" philosophers who say that values are objective, absolute, and eternal, and others who take values to be subjective, relative, and transitory. This battle goes back to the ancient Greek philosopher Plato's influential *Republic*, in which we read of the philosopher Socrates'* arguing with a public intellectual called Thrasymachus.* Hegel's phenomenological* method represents an attempt to acknowledge that values change within social and historical contexts without succumbing to relativism (the idea that points of view have no absolute truth).

## NOTES

1   G. W. F. Hegel, *Phenomenology of Spirit,* trans. A. V. Miller (Oxford: Oxford University Press, 1977), 185.

2   Henry Silton Harris, *Hegel's Ladder* (Cambridge: Hackett, 1997), 795–865.

3   Michael Quante, *Hegel's Concept of Action*, trans. Dean Moyar (Cambridge: Cambridge University Press, 2004).

# MODULE 7
# ACHIEVEMENT

## KEY POINTS

- Hegel wanted to write an introduction to what he called "philosophical science," namely his own system, and especially to his "Science of Logic."

- Hegel set out his ideas in a logical, methodical way but claimed that they could not be understood until the whole thing had been digested.

- Hegel's ideas were so complicated that they were open to interpretation. Two camps, dubbed "left" and "right," soon sprung up with radically different emphases and interpretations.

### Assessing the Argument

G. W. F. Hegel intended his *Phenomenology of Spirit* to serve as an introduction to a system of his own called "philosophical science," and especially to his "Science of Logic." As such, *Phenomenology* has at least two main aims. The first is to bring the reader to see the necessity of philosophical science. Hegel wanted to show that neither everyday consciousness nor the philosophical tradition was capable of properly understanding the relationship between the mind and the world. Hegel called this the "standpoint of the consciousness."*

The second aim was to bring the reader to what he called the "standpoint of science."[1] Here, understanding will then be replaced by "reason" and the rational structure of actuality, of what exists "in truth," can be revealed. This process of revealing the rational form of actuality—of what Hegel calls "the Absolute"* or "the Idea"—is

> ❝ According to Hegel—to use the Marxist terminology—Religion is only an ideological superstructure that is born and exists solely in relation to a real substructure. This substructure, which supports both religion and philosophy, is nothing but the totality of human actions realized during the course of universal history, that history in and by which man has created a series of specifically human worlds, essentially different from the natural world. It is these social worlds that are reflected in the religious and philosophical ideologies, and therefore—to come to the point at once—absolute knowledge, which reveals the totality of being, can be realized only at the end of history, in the last world created by man. ❞
>
> Alexandre Kojève, *Introduction to the Reading of Hegel: Lectures on the Phenomenology of Spirit*

the aim of Hegel's *Science of Logic*; it is not the aim of *Phenomenology*. Nevertheless, by attaining the standpoint of science, the reader can be assured that the world is fundamentally rational. In this sense we can see that Hegel's achievement within *Phenomenology* is necessarily limited. The text is in effect an introduction to a wider philosophical debate.

*Phenomenology* therefore is a tool-set designed to equip its reader with the necessary skills to follow Hegel into later works. Nevertheless, as the text unfolds Hegel's attempt to construct a philosophical science reveals insights, among them the master-slave dialectic,* which were to have a profound effect on both academic thought and real-world politics. Hegel fulfilled his belief that philosophical science is not only necessary but also capable of having a real impact on the world.

### Achievement in Context

The historical context within which Hegel's *Phenomenology of Spirit* was written is critical to its understanding—although perhaps not in obvious ways. The sheer complexity of the text made it inaccessible to most contemporary readers; time was needed not only to digest its content but also to allow its ideas to filter into wider circles. Divisions over its importance characterized the battles between "right" and "left" or "young" Hegelians* in the decades after his death in 1831.

"Right" Hegelians saw Hegel's later works as providing an intellectual justification for the status quo, the contemporary political and religious order. "Left" Hegelians on the other hand embraced *Phenomenology* for its stress on historical change and its critical potential. As a young man, the philosopher Karl Marx* was deeply influenced by Hegel's dialectical* method and his emphasis on the role of labor in the development of consciousness. Marxist thought in the twentieth century has frequently engaged with Hegel, especially since the 1960s when the Marxist philosopher Louis Althusser* identified a Hegelian and humanist early Marx.

In this sense we can see the importance of the context within which *Phenomenology* was written. It helped to describe modernity as it was seen from the perspective of 1807. In this period of political upheaval Hegel saw the potential for an endpoint to historical change. It was this very upheaval that made the text so compelling. After 1815, many of the so-called gains of the French Revolution* (the period between 1789 and 1799 in which France's monarchy was overthrown and a republic declared, with political and social repercussions throughout Europe), were reversed and the map of Europe was largely returned to its prerevolutionary borders. Such reversals of the "direction" of history only added fuel to the debate.

## Limitations

Hegel's thought was certainly not limited to the period in which he was writing. The spirit of revolution that had found expression in both the American Revolutionary War* (in which the young United States fought against the forces of the British Empire for their independence) and the French Revolution had certainly revealed aspects of modernity that were unique to their times. Few individual works of philosophy have been so fertile or liable to swing in and out of fashion as *Phenomenology of Spirit*. While it is still relevant more than 200 years after its publication, the nature of that relevance has varied according to the time and location of its supporters. Much so-called "continental" philosophy,* (a set of nineteenth- and twentieth-century philosophies from mainland Europe), especially from World War II* onward, has been virtually impossible to understand without Hegel.

One central reason for this is that a number of leading French intellectuals attended the philosopher Alexandre Kojève's* lectures on *Phenomenology* in the 1930s.[2] Kojève's distinctive reading of the text drew heavily on Karl Marx and the German philosopher Martin Heidegger's* phenomenology* (in the sense of "an inquiry into the nature of consciousness"). This should not be confused with "phenomenology" as Hegel used the term. Hegel, for example, emphasized the master-slave dialectic and the themes of psychological integrity and the self's quest for completion. Among the attendees were the sociologist Raymond Aron,* the philosopher Jean-Paul Sartre,* and the psychoanalyst Jacques Lacan.*

Sartre's masterpiece *Being and Nothingness* is filled with Hegelian terms and ideas, such as the relation between "being-for-self and being-for-others" in his analysis of the phenomenology of human relations. Lacan, who was also deeply affected by the philosopher Jean Hyppolite's commentary on *Phenomenology*,[3] took ideas from Hyppolite when he came to propose his own theory of the development of the psyche. Politically speaking, it was Marx and not Hegel who dominated twentieth-century history. Although the collapse of the Soviet Union* and its obvious failings in the period following World War II caused some, notably the political theorist Francis Fukuyama,* to reassess Kojève's interpretation of Hegel and reapply it to the late twentieth century.

## NOTES

1   G. F. W. Hegel, *Phenomenology of Spirit,* trans. A. V. Miller (Oxford: Oxford University Press, 1977), 50.

2   Alexandre Kojève, *Introduction to the Reading of Hegel: Lectures on the Phenomenology of Spirit*, trans. James H. Nichols, Jr. (New York: Basic Books, 1969).

3   See Jean Hyppolite, *Genesis and Structure of Hegel's* Phenomenology of Spirit, trans. Samuel Cherniak and John Heckman (Evanston: Northwestern University Press, 1974).

## MODULE 8
# PLACE IN THE AUTHOR'S WORK

### KEY POINTS

- Hegel was attempting to create a scientific method of differentiating between what we perceive as reality and what is actually real.

- Opinion is divided on whether or not *Phenomenology* represents an introduction to Hegel's ideas or can be viewed as a standalone text.

- *Phenomenology* is Hegel's best-known work. It certainly marked him as an important philosopher.

### Positioning

In terms of its content, G. W. F. Hegel's *Phenomenology* is in many ways the work of a mature scholar. His philosophy of the Absolute* was a continuation of prior thought that philosophers such as his former roommate Friedrich Wilhelm Joseph Schelling* had also tackled. Hegel's departure from Schelling can be traced to two of Hegel's earlier works: *The Difference between Fichte's and Schelling's Systems of Philosophy* (1801) and *Faith and Knowledge* (1802). It was, however, in *Phenomenology* that these differences were made clear and examined at length. Hegel argued that the Absolute was not a static being or principle, but was rather a process. His Absolute cannot be understood as an immediate, simple object of thought. Instead, it is a process of change and development driven by the internal principle he called "negation."

Nevertheless, there are fundamental differences between the philosophy he developed during his time in the city of Jena, including *Phenomenology*, and his mature system. His Jena philosophy

> **"To be radical is to grasp things by the root."**
> Karl Marx, *Critique of Hegel's "Philosophy of Right"*

emphasized the role played by human social activity in creating ways of being intelligible. But his mature system saw individual subjects swallowed up by a grand logical system in which they are just appearances.[1]

The German scholar Hans Friedrich Fulda,* among others, has pointed out that Hegel's *Encyclopedia* contains a section entitled, "Phenomenology of Spirit," which revises the ideas of the first four chapters of the 1807 *Phenomenology*, suggesting that Hegel had abandoned the early work.[2] Not everyone agreed with this interpretation, however. Scholars such as the American academic Michael N. Forster* argue that Hegel always saw *Phenomenology* as the introduction to his system.[3]

## Integration

Hegel's major works after *Phenomenology* clearly form part of what is intended to be a complete, self-contained philosophical system. This system is laid out in the three parts of Hegel's *Encyclopedia of the Philosophical Sciences* (1817; second edition 1827; third edition 1830), comprising a "logic," a philosophy of nature,* and a philosophy of mind. Hegel also published a larger version of his *Science of Logic* (first part 1812; second part 1813; third part 1816), which is the foundation of the system; and a political philosophy, *Elements of the Philosophy of Right* (1821), which is meant as an elaboration of the "Objective Spirit" section of the *Encyclopedia*.[4] Debate continues today as to whether the philosophy of *Phenomenology* is compatible with the mature system and, if it is, what relation they are meant to have with each other. Political events clearly had an effect on Hegel's thought process. For example, *Phenomenology* was completed just as Napoleon Bonaparte* defeated the Prussian army at the Battle of Jena.* Centuries of tradition were swept aside and the political landscape of Europe seemed to have been changed forever. Napoleon's eventual defeat in 1815 enabled the victorious nations to return much of Europe to its pre-French Revolution* borders but the Holy Roman Empire* was never again seen in Europe. The finality of its destruction was absolute.

### Significance

*Phenomenology* remains Hegel's most influential work and his finest book. The sheer originality of its method, its conception of philosophy as a reflection of human history, and its famous arguments for the community rather than the individual as the basic subject of thought and action have all accounted for its enduring importance. *Phenomenology*, whether it is viewed as an introduction to his later work or as a work of individual importance, certainly improved Hegel's standing in philosophical circles. It not only marked a significant departure from contemporary thought; it also raised the stakes in terms of scope and ambition.

*Phenomenology* was "so detailed and rich that it amounts to an examination of the possibility and viability of an actual historical form of life, a historical experience conducted under the assumption of such competencies and their inter-relationship."[5] It has inspired dozens of later scholars as politically diverse as Karl Marx* and Francis Fukuyama* and inspired a school of thought—Hegelianism. The ideas contained in *Phenomenology* gave rise to Historicism,* a philosophy emphasizing the historical development of society that was to have a major impact on the political evolution of Europe and the world.

# NOTES

1   See Michael Theunissen, *Hegels Lehre Vom Absoluten Geist Als Theologisch-Politischer Traktat* (Berlin: de Gruyter, 1970).

2   See Hans Friedrich Fulda, *Das Problem einer Einleitung in Hegels Wissenschaft der Logik* (Frankfurt am Main: Klostermann, 1965).

3   Michael N. Forster, *Hegel's Idea of a Phenomenology of Spirit* (Chicago: University of Chicago Press, 1998), Part 5.

4   See G. W. F. Hegel, *The Science of Logic: 1, Encyclopedia of the Philosophical Sciences*, trans. William Wallace (US: Hythloday Press, 2014); Hegel, *The Science of Logic*, trans. George Di Giovanni (Cambridge: Cambridge University Press, 2015); Hegel, *Elements of the Philosophy of Right*, trans. H. B. Nisbet and ed. Allen Wood (Cambridge: Cambridge University Press, 1991).

5   Robert B. Pippin, *Hegel on Self Consciousness* (Princeton, NJ: Princeton University Press, 2011), 2.

# SECTION 3
## IMPACT

# THE FIRST RESPONSES

## KEY POINTS

- Hegel was accused of having returned to the rationalism\* of the philosophers Gottfried Wilhelm Leibniz\* and Christian Wolff.\* *Phenomenology* was also seen by some as "incomprehensible" due to its complexity.

- The arguments that Hegel overestimated the power of conceptual theorizing and that he tried to combine highly abstract thought with historical development have both endured.

- The complexity of the text seems to have baffled many contemporary thinkers, leading to criticisms based on misunderstandings.

### Criticism

A handful of reviews of G. W. F. Hegel's *Phenomenology of Spirit* appeared in the first few years following its publication. The reviewers were united, both in their verdict that Hegel's style was extremely dense and obscure, and in their general misunderstanding of the book; no critical agreement was reached though.

Many of the book's harsher critics were doubtless taking revenge for the scathing and frequently sarcastic reviews their books had received in the *Critical Journal of Philosophy;* they might not have been certain Hegel wrote the attacks but they certainly suspected he was involved. One of the criticisms leveled was that Hegel had simply returned to the philosophical approach of rationalism of the thinkers Gottfried Wilhelm Leibniz and Christian Wolff, which had dominated German philosophy for most of the eighteenth

**❝I am nothing but I must be everything.❞**
Karl Marx, *Critique of Hegel's "Philosophy of Right"*

century. (According to the rational approach, knowledge can only be achieved through reason.) A review from 1809 in the *Allgemeine Literatur-Zeitung* ("General Literary Times"), for example, argued that Hegel had made a fundamental error pointed out by Kant: namely that we could gain definitive knowledge of objects just through using formal logic.[1] Had Hegel, it asked, not understood a central point of the Kantian revolution, that our concepts have meaning only in relation to sensory experience?

Other reviewers simply found it incomprehensible. A review from *Neue Leipzig Literaturzeitung* ("New Leipzig Literary Times"), for instance, failed to see how Hegel could show that the shapes of consciousness he surveyed were one-sided, suppressing aspects of their true selves theoretically opposed to their own essence.[2] The reviewer, therefore, claimed that the book was littered with contradictions. He pointed to Hegel's claim that the truth of the master's consciousness is the slave's. Instead of seeing how this claim pointed to the need for master and slave to recognize one another as equals, the reviewer simply took it as a contradiction.[3]

## Responses

The misunderstandings the critics displayed were so fundamental they hardly deserved detailed responses. Two particularly crude criticisms of G. W. F. Hegel's *Phenomenology of Spirit* have enjoyed an enduring shelf life. The review from 1807 in the *Oberdeutsche Allgemeine Literaturzeitung* ("South German General Literary Newspaper") mistook Hegel's philosophy for a version of that of the philosopher Fichte.[4] Yet in doing so the reviewer complained that Hegel overestimated the power of theorizing and failed to acknowledge that certain things might be unknowable and therefore one would be unable to categorize them systematically. Critics have since frequently leveled the charge that Hegel swallows up all reality in his theory of the Absolute.

The philosopher J. F. Fries* disliked *Phenomenology* because of its "unpalatable language,"[5] adding that the whole thing was completely contradictory since it declared all knowledge to be in flux and relative while at the same time suggesting it spoke from an absolute standpoint.[6] While the charge of relativism is crude and misplaced, Hegel's attempt to combine metaphysics* with historical development has continually presented an obstacle to his readers.

## Conflict and Consensus

Nevertheless, Hegel's developing conception of his own philosophy does not owe anything to contemporary critiques of *Phenomenology*. After the Napoleonic invasion of Jena the city was largely in ruins, many fled, and the university could barely function. Hegel left the city and did not become a university professor until 1816. In 1807 he went to the town of Bamberg to edit a pro-Napoleonic newspaper and in 1808 he became rector of a gymnasium (a type of secondary school) in Nuremberg. These demanding activities, following so soon after the publication of *Phenomenology*, are another reason why his philosophical development did not come from dialogue with his early critics.

Much more formative was the experience of using *Phenomenology* as a text for his teaching at the gymnasium. Doing so forced him to reconsider the status of the text within his system and its adequacy as an introduction to that system.

The teaching guidelines set by his friend Friedrich Immanuel Niethammer*—the Commissioner of Education in Bavaria— specified an "Introduction to Knowledge of the Universal Coherence of the Sciences." From this, Hegel understood that he was to teach how the different philosophical sciences were logically interrelated. With this in mind, he produced what he called an "encyclopedia" of his emerging system as a basis for teaching.

Hegel eventually integrated the first sections of *Phenomenology* into this encyclopedia, which became the basis for his mature system. The phenomenological sections established the standpoint of "universal consciousness," which was needed for a more detailed philosophy of spirit. This philosophy would then serve as the basis for the standpoint for his logic of basic ontological* categories* and for his "real philosophy," that is, his philosophy of nature* and spirit. The fact that the historical sections of *Phenomenology* did not appear in their earlier form had, in fact, very little to do with criticisms the text had received.

## NOTES

1 Friedhelm Nicolin (ed.), *Hegel in Berichten Seiner Zeitgenossen* (Hamburg: Felix Meiner Verlag, 1970), 87.

2 Wolfgang Bonsiepen, "Erste Zeitgenössische Rezensionen der Phänomenologie des Geistes," *Hegel-Studien* 14 (1979): 28–30.

3 Bonsiepen, "Erste Zeitgenössische Rezensionen," 30.

4 Bonsiepen, "Erste Zeitgenössische Rezensionen," 30.

5 Stephen Houlgate, *Hegel's "Phenomenology of Spirit": A Reader's Guide* (London & New York: Bloomsbury Publishing, 2013), 191.

6 Terry Pinkard, *Hegel: A Biography* (New York: Cambridge University Press, 2000), 261.

# MODULE 10
## THE EVOLVING DEBATE

### KEY POINTS

- Of all Hegel's ideas, his linking of philosophical thought to the progression of history has had the most impact both in the abstract world of philosophy and in the real world of politics.

- The initial "left" and "right" Hegelians gave way to more complex schools of thought. Neo-Kantianism,* Marxism,* and positivism* all owe some debt to Hegel, even if they oppose his thoughts. The most significant school is, however, the one directly related to Hegel— "Hegelianism."

- Hegel's thoughts were for a time overshadowed by the theories of Karl Marx,* which changed the political landscape of the world for almost an entire century. With the collapse of the Soviet Union,* thinkers such as Francis Fukuyama* reclaimed Hegel.

### Uses and Problems

Due to the complexity of G. W. F. Hegel's *Phenomenology of Spirit*, what passes for "Hegelian" is often simply what has been labeled "Hegelian" by his interpreters and critics. Tracing the influence of *Phenomenology of Spirit* on the evolution of philosophical debate requires careful sorting through the representations and misrepresentations of both its supporters and critics.

Hegel's great legacy has been the idea that history is essential to philosophy, and *Phenomenology* has remained the central text for those seeking to exploit this key Hegelian idea. *Phenomenology* is one

> ❝ For the nature of humanity is to impel men to agree with one another, and its very existence lies simply in the explicit realization of a community of conscious life. ❞
>
> G. W. F. Hegel, *The Phenomenology of Spirit*

of the main "game changers" not just of modern philosophy, but of Western philosophy as a whole.

For many in philosophy, and especially for thinkers in the humanities, Hegel's famous contention that philosophy is "its own time captured in thought"[1] represents an intellectual point of no return. Intellectual theorizing can be understood only as it emerges from its background historical conditions, be they social, economic, or political. In terms of the text's evolution one must be cautious. Hegel's methodology was both unfinished and open to interpretation. Philosophers such as Karl Marx and Alexandre Kojève* did not complete the work—they either adapted or reinterpreted it.

## Schools of Thought

Considerable historical and interpretative care is needed when attempting to understand the philosophical camps that formed in the decades after Hegel's death in 1831. The "right" Hegelians, whose influence on subsequent philosophy has been small, took themselves to be bearers of Hegelian orthodoxy. Often politically conservative, their view that the mid-nineteenth-century Prussian state was the peak of European civilization was not to stand the test of history.

The "left" or "young" Hegelians,* especially Ludwig Feuerbach* and Karl Marx, however, have had an enormous intellectual impact. Marx's influential theory of economic change, which he called "dialectical materialism," for example, adapts several elements of Hegel's theory of dialectical development. These philosophers would, however, set themselves up as severe critics of what they saw as Hegel's idealism* and theoretical method. Current scholarship, though, clearly shows that their dismissals of Hegel rely on caricatures and their own positive views remain deeply indebted to his work.[2]

Similarly, large-scale philosophical movements have been born as reactions to so-called "Hegelian Idealism." Both the positivist* and neo-Kantian schools of philosophy and social science that emerged in the mid-nineteenth century were reactions to the apparent threat of Hegelian Idealism. Likewise, the empiricist* nature of early twentieth-century analytic philosophy, with its emphasis on the necessity of verifiable evidence comes from a reaction to another false representation of Hegelianism. In this case, it was the reaction of the philosophers G. E. Moore* and Bertrand Russell* to the theoretical excesses of the British idealists active in the late nineteenth and early twentieth centuries.

### In Current Scholarship

Recent "non-metaphysical" readings of G. W. F. Hegel have inspired new thinking among key contemporary philosophers. In particular, University of Pittsburgh philosophers John McDowell* and Robert Brandom* and their followers are only half-jokingly known as the "Pittsburgh Hegelians." For both, *Phenomenology of Spirit* has been their almost exclusive object of study.[3]

McDowell and Brandom are adapting select themes of *Phenomenology* and modernizing them through current analytic techniques. In particular, they read Hegel through the ideas of the American philosopher Wilfrid Sellars,* whose famous essay "Empiricism and the Philosophy of Mind" was initially subtitled "Meditations Hegeliennes."[4]

Contemporary political philosophy also shows a self-conscious

Hegelian influence. This can be seen in critiques of such classics of twentieth-century liberal philosophy as John Rawls's* *A Theory of Justice*.[5] Thinkers associated with communitarian* political philosophy, such as Michael Sandel* and Michael Walzer,* challenge some of Rawls's work, for example the idea that the main task of a political philosophy is to justify methods for distributing goods or securing a private space in which individuals can pursue their own ends.

While communitarianism* (a social philosophy emphasizing the links between individual and community) is generally thought to have its philosophical roots in the Greek philosopher Aristotle* and Hegel, its representatives do not necessarily work with Hegel's actual texts. Nevertheless, critics of liberalism* (a political philosophy founded on the importance of individual liberty) such as Charles Taylor* and Alasdair MacIntyre*, who are sympathetic toward communitarianism to some degree, are deeply involved with Hegel's texts.

MacIntyre and especially Taylor have made important contributions to our understanding of *Phenomenology*. Both are influenced by Hegel's historicist* notion of rationality and the logic of dialectical* historical development the text proposes. MacIntyre and Taylor also emphasize the importance of rationality to communities and traditions. More recently, Robert Pippin,* although no critic of political liberalism, has written strong critiques of certain dominant Rawlsian* and Kantian trends in modern political and moral philosophy, through his sophisticated interpretation of Hegel.

## NOTES

1   Cited in Rasmus Ugilt, *The Metaphysics of Terror: The Incoherent System of Contemporary Politics,* (London & New York: Bloomsbury Academic, 2012), 27.

2   Karl Ameriks, "The Legacy of Idealism in the Philosophy of Feuerbach, Marx, and Kierkegaard," in *The Cambridge Companion to German Idealism*, ed. Karl Ameriks (Cambridge: Cambridge University Press, 2000), 258–82.

3   See John McDowell, *Having the World in View: Essays on Kant, Hegel, and Schelling* (London: Harvard University Press, 2009); and Robert Brandom, *Tales of the Mighty Dead: Historical Essays in the Metaphysics of Intentionality* (London: Harvard University Press, 2002).

4   See Wilfrid Sellars, "Empiricism and the Philosophy of Mind," in *Minnesota Studies in the Philosophy of Science, Volume I: The Foundations of Science and the Concepts of Psychology and Psychoanalysis*, eds. Herbert Feigl and Michael Scriven (University of Minnesota Press, 1956), 253–329.

5   John Rawls, *A Theory of Justice* (Cambridge, MA: Harvard University Press, 1971).

# MODULE 11
# IMPACT AND INFLUENCE TODAY

## KEY POINTS

- Two broad camps exist, split roughly between the Anglo-Americans and the Continental Europeans. The latter are less suspicious of Hegel's attempts to create ideas that are systematically complete.

- Although Hegel's work is of immense significance, it remains one of the most difficult texts to understand in all philosophy. Major arguments continue over its metaphysical* and non-metaphysical meaning.

- Idealist* philosophers claim that Hegel successfully continued Immanuel Kant's* work. But those leaning toward Hegelian metaphysics claim that his work is a continuation of pre-Kantian ideas that stretch back to the philosophers Leibniz* and even Aristotle.*

### Position

The power of *Phenomenology* to offer philosophical inspiration can be seen in its fate in anglophone* (English–speaking) "analytic" philosophy.* It was abandoned by anglophone philosophers after Bertrand Russell* and G. E. Moore* rejected the "Hegelianism" of their British idealist teachers and created analytic philosophy. Since the early 1990s, however, some major figures in analytic philosophy have started to engage with *Phenomenology*. Some of these, such as Robert Brandom,* are in the American pragmatist* tradition. Few could have anticipated such a philosophical marriage. Indeed, William James,* a founder of pragmatism, claimed to have understood Hegel only while under the influence of laughing gas.

> **"** Indeed, we all know that the man who attentively contemplates a thing, who wants to see it as it is without changing anything, is 'absorbed,' so to speak, by this contemplation—i.e., by this thing. He forgets himself, he thinks only about the thing being contemplates; he thinks neither about his contemplation, nor—and even less—about himself, his 'I,' his Selbst.* The more he is conscious of the thing, the less he is conscious of himself. He may perhaps talk about the thing, but he will never talk about himself; in his discourse, the word 'I' will not occur. For this word to appear, something other than purely passive contemplation, which only reveals being, must also be present. And this other thing, according to Hegel, is Desire. **"**
>
> Alexandre Kojève, *Introduction to the Reading of Hegel: Lectures on the Phenomenology of Spirit*

Contemporary interest in *Phenomenology* can also be seen in the output of some prominent philosophers working within the field of critical theory,* a branch of philosophy rooted in the analysis of contemporary society. Several of the text's key concepts, especially alienation* and recognition,* are seen as useful tools for contemporary social criticism. The scholar Axel Honneth,* for example, has combined these with insights from psychoanalysis and the contemporary philosophy of language.[1]

## Interaction

Philosophers today, lacking faith in Hegelian demands for systematic completeness or for thinking without presupposing, have distanced themselves from one of his central intentions. Anglo-American philosophy in particular is characterized by a suspicion of grand systematizing. Instead, it believes in a piecemeal approach to philosophy that deals with specific philosophical and technical problems.

Only in continental Europe, perhaps thanks to the philosopher Martin Heidegger,* has Hegel's systematization remained influential. Nevertheless, specific Hegelian ideas, if not their systematic ambition, continue to challenge the intellectual environment. In continental philosophy,* Hegel became a key philosophical reference point as *Phenomenology* became the key Hegelian text. This was driven by the fact that its importance for Karl Marx's* philosophy was becoming clear.

In the Anglo-American world, *Phenomenology* had to overcome two main challenges. First, Hegel's name was synonymous with the philosophical systematizing of the past. Second, there were political reasons for avoiding Hegel. During World War II* and the Cold War,* Hegel was associated respectively with German nationalism* and with the Marxism* and communism that his work inadvertently inspired. Classic statements of political suspicion toward Hegel are found in the political theorist Isaiah Berlin's* 1958 lecture "Two Concepts of Liberty" and the Austrian British philosopher Karl Popper's* *The Open Society and its Enemies* of 1945.[2]

Regarding the first challenge, the grounds for an appreciation of Hegel's ideas were laid by a gradual resurgence in Kantian idealism,* which, as we have seen, is a philosophy founded on the notion that reality is constructed in the mind. The work of philosophers such as Peter Strawson* was crucial here. Strawson used the Kantian idea of fundamental conceptual schemes* underlying our interpretation of the world as a way to correct the prevailing empiricism.*[3] Such work paved the way for the exploration of post-Kantian* idealism, especially Hegel's, that we see today and that builds on the idea of a conceptual scheme.

Regarding the second challenge, philosophers such as Charles Taylor* and Shlomo Avineri* wrote important works on Hegel in the

1970s that did much to explain the true nature of his political work. Taylor emphasized that, far from being proto-totalitarian,* Hegel's political vision was intended to preserve the rights and liberties of Enlightenment* thought. It also tried to explain how individuals could view the state as more than just a means of safeguarding a private sphere.[4]

## The Continuing Debate

A debate has arisen within the scholarly community since the early 1990s among those studying Hegel and German idealism. It is usually characterized as taking place between supporters of "metaphysical" and supporters of "non-metaphysical" interpretations of Hegel, although many of the participants would reject these labels.

The non-metaphysical reading challenges the received view that Hegel is a traditional metaphysician who returns to pre-Kantian rationalism—that is, to philosophy as it was practiced in Europe prior to Kant's critique* of metaphysics. For supporters of the metaphysical view, Hegel belongs to a philosophical tradition for which being and reality are open to analysis by the rational intellect, a tradition whose roots go back through Leibniz all the way to Aristotle.

Non-metaphysical views, such as that put forward in the American philosopher Robert Pippin's* *Hegel's Idealism: The Satisfactions of Self-Consciousness* (1991), take seriously Hegel's claim to have completed Kant's philosophical revolution.[5] Hegel's absolute idealism, so these interpreters claim, continues the workings of Kant. In other words, Hegel's philosophy is not an uncritical inquiry into the nature of being; rather it is an exploration of the extent to which our finite minds can comprehend the universe and our experience of it.

While this issue is really just a skirmish within the narrow world of Hegel studies, it has made clear the stakes involved in the heated question of contemporary philosophy's relation to its history. Critics (for example, Frederick Beiser*) of the recent attempt to portray

Hegel as initiating a Kantian-influenced investigation into the grounds of what we know attack interpreters such as Robert Pippin and Terry Pinkard* for not being faithful to Hegel's intentions and for ignoring his wider work.[6] Writers such as Beiser are motivated in part by a worry that if we read past philosophers too much in our own image and in the light of current concerns, we lose sight of the original challenges they faced and the insights they can give us.

In addition, there has been a general tendency of philosophy from the English-speaking world to fall into two camps, which the American philosopher Richard Rorty* labeled "rational" and "historical reconstruction." Both camps tend to exercise a kind of historical neutrality, as if the work (as the British thinker Gilbert Ryle* noted) had been published in last week's philosophical journals.[7]

## NOTES

1   Axel Honneth, *The Struggle for Recognition*, trans. Joel Anderson (Cambridge: Polity Press, 1995).

2   Isaiah Berlin, *Four Essays on Liberty* (Oxford: Oxford University Press, 1969); Karl Popper, *The Open Society and Its Enemies, Vol. 2, The High Tide of Prophecy: Hegel, Marx, and the Aftermath* (London: Routledge, 1952).

3   Peter Strawson, *Bounds of Sense: An Essay on Kant's* Critique of Pure Reason (London: Methuen, 1966).

4   Charles Taylor, *Hegel* (Cambridge: Cambridge University Press, 1975); Shlomo Avineri, *Hegel's Theory of the Modern State* (Cambridge: Cambridge University Press, 1972).

5   Robert B. Pippin, *Hegel's Idealism: The Satisfactions of Self-Consciousness* (Cambridge: Cambridge University Press, 1989).

6   Frederick Beiser, "Dark Days: Anglophone Scholarship Since the 1960s," in *German Idealism: Contemporary Perspectives*, ed. Espen Hammer (Abingdon: Routledge, 2007), 70–91.

7   Richard Rorty, "The Historiography of Philosophy: Four Genres," in *Philosophy in History,* eds. Richard Rorty, J. B. Schneewind, and Quentin Skinner (Cambridge: Cambridge University Press, 1984), 31–49.

# MODULE 12
# WHERE NEXT?

## KEY POINTS

- Since the collapse of communism in 1991, the theories of Karl Marx* have fallen from grace. This has created a renewed interest in Hegel that cuts across traditional political factions.

- Hegel's masterpiece will continue to inspire, not least because its inaccessibility gives great scope for interpretation.

- Hegel began debates that continue today. The sheer breadth of his ideas influenced political philosophy for centuries. His influence on Marx has seen the world's political landscape shift in numerous, radical ways.

### Potential

Much of G. W. F. Hegel's mature thought, particularly that published after *Phenomenology of Spirit*, receives relatively little attention. This is partly due to changes in the philosophical climate. Hegel's *Science of Logic* (1812–16), which lays out the conceptual structure of the Absolute, seems to exist in a parallel philosophical universe to contemporary philosophy, which prefers a piecemeal approach and uses a logic developed in the early twentieth century.[1] But philosophical fashion is fickle and Hegel's speculative logic might well have an unexpected future. When it comes to the political philosophy of the "Philosophy of Right," however, much of its content simply belongs to a bygone age. The political realities of early nineteenth-century Prussia are long gone.

Few today believe that *Phenomenology* can possess the significance

**❝**For Hegel ... liberal society is a reciprocal and equal agreement among citizens to mutually recognize each other.**❞**

Francis Fukuyama, *The End of History and the Last Man*

Hegel intended since it was supposed to be a justification for (and was governed by) his logic. Likewise, contemporary social and political realities mean that key concepts of *Phenomenology* can have at best limited application.

Yet in spite of historical change and philosophical fashion, *Phenomenology* has had a remarkable ability to retain its relevance. Of course, much of its popularity in the twentieth century has been due to its connection with Marxism.* Yet the decline of Marxism has not been mirrored by a decline in interest in *Phenomenology*. Quite the opposite: philosophers are now looking back at the text with fresh eyes and not as a means simply to support the ideas of a different philosophical theory.

### Future Directions

*Phenomenology* looks set to continue to be a source of insights for philosophers of all kinds. Those, for example, who believe that knowledge does not come exclusively through the senses but instead requires forms of conceptual mediation, are always going to be drawn to Hegel's arguments. *Phenomenology* is also likely to remain the seminal text for those philosophers who see an essential connection between theory and practice, philosophical developments, and the historical time in which they emerged.

Finally, however different our societies are from Hegel's own, many philosophers still say that it is Hegel who best understands the conflicts of value that underlie the modern world. The Canadian philosopher Charles Taylor*, in his classic book *Hegel* (1975) and later in his *Sources of the Self* (1989),[2] argues that we are caught between two sources of value: rational autonomy*—the idea that each individual can direct his or her own life through his or her own reason—and what Taylor called "expressive unity," the need to see one's self expressed in wider wholes, for example, works of art, religious practices, or the community. Suggesting one is more important than the other, as so much contemporary moral and political philosophy does, cannot do justice to the different goods essential to modern identity. Hegel, Taylor argues, has given us the most sophisticated account of this conflict and its historical sources. If we do not agree with Hegel's solutions, we must first clarify the reasons for that disagreement and then face the problems he diagnosed ourselves.

## Summary

*Phenomenology* is in many respects a product of its age. Although produced at a time of radical revolutions in Europe, it was nevertheless written within the context of the Holy Roman Empire,* a political institution founded in the Middle Ages. Hegel shared the opinion of his contemporaries that philosophy must form a system derivable from a single principle, a belief that can seem odd to contemporary minds. Yet of all the philosophical works of the period, indeed of the nineteenth century as a whole, *Phenomenology* has enjoyed the most interest and influence.

Today, its ideas provide inspiration for projects not only in fields familiar to Hegel, such as the theory of knowledge, but also in areas to which he paid little attention, or that simply did not exist in his time, such as the philosophy of language. Similarly, many of the book's key concepts, such as alienation* or recognition,* continue to be developed within political thought and social criticism. These fields are currently reexamining the contributions of *Phenomenology*, as it emerges from the Marxist context in which it has sat for most of the twentieth century.

The sheer variety of topics in *Phenomenology* and its attempt to integrate them within one philosophical vision makes it a work without comparison. Hegel's attempt to write a developmental history of Western consciousness that includes and connects its central philosophical and cultural moments has never been equaled. Its novel method of immanent critique, on the other hand, in which a position is criticized by its own internal standards and assumptions, continues to breed imitators in a variety of fields.

Perhaps most important of all, *Phenomenology* is often viewed as the text in which Hegel does most to pursue the idea that sets his thought apart from previous philosophy: namely, that philosophical truth is essentially developmental and is therefore one and the same as its emergence in historical time. For contemporary Hegelians, this is a lesson that today's philosophy would to do well to learn, even if the prospects of somebody writing a *Phenomenology of Spirit: Part 2*, extending Hegel's text from the early nineteenth to the early twenty-first century, look dim indeed.

## NOTES

1   G. W. F. Hegel, *The Science of Logic*, trans. George Di Giovanni (Cambridge: Cambridge University Press, 2015).

2   Charles Taylor, *Hegel* (Cambridge: Cambridge University Press, 1975); Taylor, *Sources of the Self: The Making of the Modern Identity* (Cambridge: Cambridge University Press, 1989).

# GLOSSARIES

# GLOSSARY OF TERMS

**Absolute:** for Hegel, the Absolute was that which was independent and unchanging, an absolute truth that is inherently unknowable—though the process of attempting to understand it can aid our understanding of the whole.

**Alienation:** process whereby individuals begin to see the world around them as alien. According to Hegel, culture was created through the actions of people but over time it became alien to them. Karl Marx saw this aspect of Hegel's thought as crucial to an understanding of history. The two men differed greatly on this point. For Hegel, culture was an expression of the Spirit; for Marx, culture was a product of human labour.

**Analytic philosophy/Continental philosophy:** a school of Western philosophy from the early twentieth century onward that is often divided into "analytic" and "continental" schools. Analytic philosophy has chiefly been practiced in Anglophone countries and continental philosophy in mainland Europe, with France and Germany as notable centers. Although this terminological distinction has common currency, few are content with any of the definitions offered to differentiate the two schools. Many argue that the differences amount to little more than variations in style, sensibility, and seminal figures and that the terms are therefore unhelpful.

**Anglophone:** someone from the English-speaking world.

**Apartheid:** a system of racial segregation that existed in South Africa between 1948 and 1994.

**Autonomy:** individuals' freedom to make decisions on their own without undue influence from outside. Kant argued that individual autonomy is an important aspect of the political and moral world in which we live. He placed weight upon the ability of individuals to govern themselves regardless of their place in society.

**Battle of Jena:** a battle fought in 1806 near the river Saale between the forces of Napoleon Bonaparte and Frederick III of Prussia. The resulting French victory broke Prussian power for the remainder of the decade.

*Bildungsroman:* the German term for a philosophical novel.

**British idealism:** a movement in British philosophy that flourished in the second half of the nineteenth century and faded in the early twentieth. Its principal originators were T. H. Green (1836–82), F. H. Bradley (1846–1924), and Bernard Bosanquet (1848–1923). British idealism was a fairly disparate movement, broadly characterized by its opposition to empiricism and utilitarianism (a doctrine that uses utility as a guiding principle, according to which an action is right if it tends to promote happiness and wrong if it tends to produce the reverse of happiness) and by its doctrines that there is one single all-inclusive reality, the Absolute, and that thought and reality are essentially united. Although the idealists adopted elements of Hegelian terminology and broad Hegelian themes, their philosophy was not fundamentally indebted to Hegel.

**Carlsbad decrees:** introduced by the German Confederation in September 1819, they dissolved the various German university fraternities to root out revolutionary sentiment and nationalism, purged the universities of liberal professors, and imposed severe restrictions on the press and academic publishing. It is often thought that the relative conservatism of Hegel's later political philosophy is in part explained by his concern for his position and fear of the censors established by the decrees.

**Categories:** Aristotle believed that all of existence fell into one of 10 categories, which were collectively known as *predicamenta*. The categories were: substance, quantity, qualification, relative, place, time, posture, condition, action, and affection. Hegel identified 11 categories: being, becoming, one, many, essence, existence, cause, effect, universal, mechanism, and "life."

**Class struggle:** refers to the tension that exists between rival socioeconomic groups and the differing wants and needs of separate classes. It is most commonly associated with Marxist ideology, although Marx himself adapted the idea from Hegel's master-slave dialectic.

**Classical Greece:** not to be confused with Ancient Greece, the classic period, also known as the Hellenic, encompassed the fifth and fourth centuries B.C.E. It marked a period of innovation in areas such as art, philosophy, architecture, and produced literature so profound that it would influence Western culture for millennia. The primary schools of Hellenistic philosophy are Stoicism, Skepticism, and Cynicism, of which the first two are discussed in the "Self-Consciousness" section of *Phenomenology*.

**Cold War**: defined as a military "tension" between the United States and the Soviet Union; it lasted from around 1945 to 1991.

**Communitarianism**: a philosophy that emphasizes the connection between a community and an individual.

**Conceptual schemes**: in *Critique of Pure Reason*, Immanuel Kant argued that the sensation and experience of an object that is received via our senses can only be understood thanks to basic concepts that he called categories. These categories help us to perceive objects as they truly are.

**Consciousness:** Hegel's concept of consciousness relied on the idea that in order truly to understand something one required more than the input provided by the senses. He identified three sub-categories within this first step of grasping the absolute: sensuous—our immediate certainty of an object; perceiving—in which we begin to unravel a thing's true nature; and understanding—in which we grasp something of its true nature. Consciousness is, however, only part of a process on the path to true knowledge and requires one to examine categories, acknowledge contradiction, and move on toward a more refined viewpoint that is one step closer to truth.

**Critical theory:** An analytical approach to culture, notably to literature, that foregrounds the ideology, historical forces, and social constraints that influenced its creation.

***Critique of Pure Reason*:** a book by the philosopher Immanuel Kant that was published in 1781 and remains one of the most influential philosophical texts of all time. In it, Kant argued that contradictions were required in order to arrive at true knowledge.

**Critique:** a term that in Kant has a technical sense that need not have negative connotations. By critique, Kant means an investigation into the grounds for, and the limits of, any *a priori* principle claimed by human knowledge. *A priori* knowledge is knowledge possessed independently of experience. Kantian critique becomes negative when it reveals a given claim to *a priori* knowledge to be more limited in scope than is generally supposed.

**Dialectic:** a method of resolving an argument between two viewpoints in order to ascertain truth. Although the dialectic itself is a concept that stretches back to ancient Greek times, Kant, Hegel, and Marx developed the idea further.

**Divine immanence:** in recent philosophy, the understanding that the Deity permanently pervades and sustains the universe; this is distinguished from the notion of an external transcendent creator or ruler.

**Doctrine of being:** according to Hegel, Kant's view that reality is shaped through the mind. Hegel continued to explore these ideas in his three-book work *The Science of Logic*, published between 1812 and 1816.

**Empiricism:** doctrine that regards experience as the only source of knowledge.

**Enlightenment:** a movement in seventeenth- and eighteenth-century Europe and North America that challenged commonly held ideas based in tradition and faith, and tried to advance knowledge through rationality and science. The movement was devoted to fighting irrationality, superstition, and arbitrary political authority.

**Epistemology:** a theory or science of the method or grounds of knowledge.

**Ethics:** the philosophy of right and wrong behavior. For Hegel, ethics represented more than a simple "right versus wrong" equation. He saw the morality that took place in normal, everyday exchanges of information as part of a wider system that he named Ethical life.

**European Renaissance:** the period of history that followed the Middle Ages. (The Middle Ages are roughly the fifth to the fifteenth centuries C.E.)

**French Revolution:** the period between 1789 and 1799 in which France's monarchy was overthrown and a republic was declared, with political and social repercussions throughout Europe.

**German Idealism:** a reaction against Kant's *Critique of Pure Reason*, German Idealism emerged during the late eighteenth century and early nineteenth century and included Hegel, J. G. Fichte, and F. W. J. Schelling as members.

**German Romanticism:** developing later than its anglophone counterpart, German Romanticism began in the late eighteenth century and early nineteenth century. It was a literary and intellectual movement that emphasized emotion as an aesthetic experience.

**Historicism:** a theory that emphasizes the role of history in society. In Hegel's view all human activities are defined by their history. Marx also adapted these ideas, which led to his understanding of history as a science, a historical process of improvement that moves inexorably, if at times gradually, toward what he described as communism.

**Holism:** the view that the parts of a system must be understood in terms of their relations to the whole. Individual parts cannot be fully understood in isolation. Holism can be applied to a vast range of fields: economic, social, biological, linguistic, epistemological, metaphysical, and so on. While Hegel's philosophy undoubtedly possesses many holistic elements, the precise nature of his holism is deeply controversial.

**Holy Roman Empire:** an affiliation of central European states of historically changing political integrity, founded in the Middle Ages and dissolved in 1806, shortly after the Battle of Jena.

**Idealism:** the idea that reality is constructed within the mind and is therefore essentially immaterial. Immanuel Kant was primarily responsible for stimulating German Idealism in the late eighteenth century.

**Identity philosophy:** a philosophical approach concerned with the meaning of identity and the changes to one's identity over a period of time.

**Incarnation theology:** a school of theology that focuses on the study of the Incarnation.

**Incarnation:** traditional doctrine in Christianity according to which the second person of the Trinity, the Son, was conceived in the Virgin Mary. (The doctrine of the Trinity suggests that God, while one, exists in three united persons: Father, Son, and Holy Spirit.) The Incarnation doctrine asserts that the "word" (*Logos*) was made flesh and that one of the divine persons of the Trinity had a fully human existence.

**Intrinsic value of nature**: according to Novalis, a German poet and philosopher, humanity was striving to return to a harmonious state with nature, one that had existed in some unspecified golden age of the past.

**Invisible church:** defined by Immanuel Kant as being one of personal faith based on rational morality as opposed to the physical church that we could "see," which was based on theological morality.

**Kantian:** adjective applied to ideas that stem from the philosopher Immanuel Kant.

**Liberalism:** a belief that government is created to promote the well-being of society. Liberalism also focuses on the rights of the individual person as a central concern.

**Marxism:** the political system advocated by Karl Marx that emphasized an end to capitalism by taking control of the means of production from private hands and placing it firmly in the hands of central government.

**Marxism-Leninism:** the political ideology of the Communist Party of the Soviet Union, based on the ideas of Karl Marx and the revolutionary leader Vladimir Ilyich Lenin.

**Master-slave dialectic:** a highly influential concept mentioned in *Phenomenology of Spirit*, the dialectic involves the recognition between two separate consciousnesses that ultimately involves a struggle in order that one dominates the other. Such a struggle is doomed, since the master's desire to be recognized as superior to the slave cannot be fulfilled since the slave is not free to offer such recognition.

**Materialism:** a philosophical idea that matter is the most important aspect of nature. Even thought is considered to be somehow related to matter; the ideas of Materialism contradict those of Idealism.

**Metaphysics**: a branch of philosophy that addresses the questions pertinent to existence, reality, or being itself.

**Modern action theory:** an area of philosophy concerned with the causes of actual willful bodily actions. For example, a hungry person standing in front of a meal may reach out to grab some food, thus satisfying a desire.

**Moral relativism:** although Kant believed that moral law was universal, it is clear that different cultures place different emphasis on moral judgments. Moral relativism, then, is a philosophy that attempts to understand and at times justify the differing morality of disparate people.

**Mutual recognition:** tied in to Hegel's master-slave dialectic, the need for mutual recognition stems from Plato's concept of *thymos*, the aspect of humanity that separates us from all other animals. It can best be understood as the part of the psyche that desires recognition as a human being; a society based on slavery, for example, is unstable since the slaves are not recognized as human beings and will eventually rise up.

**Napoleonic Wars:** a series of wars that took place between 1803 and 1815. The conflict arose from the ashes of the French Revolution and saw the French Emperor Napoleon Bonaparte pit his forces against almost every other major power in Europe.

**Nationalism:** individuals' political or ideological identification of themselves with their nation or country.

**Natural rights:** theories that specify and justify the rights individuals possess irrespective of their particular wishes and beliefs and of the customs, laws, and moral codes of their societies. Natural rights are therefore contrasted with positive or legal rights.

**Natural theology:** the branch of theology that attempts to find religious truths from common experience and natural reason. It is contrasted with revealed theology, which attempts to find religious truths from revealed scriptures or other divine interventions in the natural order.

**Neo–Kantian:** refers to a philosophical movement that took place during the mid-nineteenth century, a "return to Kant" after the philosophical school of materialism had begun to take hold.

**Noumenal:** a word Immanuel Kant used to describe something that was essentially unknowable. Hegel rejected this notion claiming that if something existed it had to be knowable.

**Ontology:** the branch of philosophy concerned with the nature of being. It is usually considered a subdiscipline of metaphysics. Ontology comprises two main tasks, both tracing their ancestry to Aristotle. One inquires into the basic categories that any kind of "being" must conform to if it is to be thinkable at all (that is, a fixed object of thought). The other inquires into what is truly real and therefore into different grades or statuses of reality.

**Pantheism:** the doctrine that God is identical with nature or the universe, most commonly associated with the philosophy of Benedictus de Spinoza.

**Patrician:** the ruling elite in ancient Rome—a group of families that held control over the empire. In modern terms, patrician politics refers to something that is oligarchic or at least inherently undemocratic.

**Phenomenology:** not to be confused with the title of Hegel's book, Phenomenology as a philosophical movement studies the experience of consciousness itself and the phenomena that occur within one's consciousness.

**Philosophy of nature** (*Naturphilosophie*): a strand of philosophical and scientific thinking that was active in late eighteenth- and early nineteenth-century Germany. It is associated especially with F. W. J. Schelling. Schelling wanted to integrate the spontaneity and reflexivity of the ego, as it had been theorized by Immanuel Kant and J. G. Fichte, into nature. Schelling's philosophy of nature emphasized the dynamic quality of nature and the importance of organic wholes. The second of the three parts of Hegel's mature *Encyclopedia of the Philosophical Sciences* is a philosophy of nature.

**Phrenology** and **Physiognomy**: an early nineteenth-century pseudoscience that tried to infer the human personality by examining facial expressions and lumps on the cranium.

**Positivism:** a philosophy that believes information derived from the senses and given a logical and mathematical treatment is the exclusive source of all knowledge.

**Post-Kantian:** not to be confused with the term neo-Kantian, which refers to thinkers later in the nineteenth century, post-Kantian refers to those ideas formulated by philosophers who followed in the immediate wake of Kant and tried to modify or adapt his ideas. Included in this group are Hegel, J. G. Fichte and F. W. J. Schelling.

**Postulates of pure practical reason:** the idea of postulates of pure practical reason features most prominently in Immanuel Kant's 1788 text *Critique of Practical Reason*. Practical postulates are theoretically improvable yet practically necessary presuppositions of moral action. Kant claims there are three postulates: freedom of the will, immortality of the soul, and the existence of God.

**Pragmatism:** a philosophical approach that originated in the latter half of the nineteenth century in the United States with such philosophers as Charles Sanders Peirce (1839–1914), William James (1842–1910), and John Dewey (1859–1952). Pragmatism's central idea is that the content of hypotheses is to be explained in terms of their practical consequences. It is commonly applied to the notion of truth, but has further application, for example, in ethics and semantics.

**Protestant:** a Christian denomination that broke free from the primacy of Roman Catholicism in the sixteenth century.

**Prussia:** a country situated in what is now northern Germany. Originally a duchy, it gradually expanded its territory until in 1701 it was reformed as the Kingdom of Prussia. The country was instrumental in the eventual unification of Germany, which occurred in 1871.

**Ratiocination:** the process of reasoning.

**Rationalism:** a prominent philosophical position in seventeenth- and eighteenth-century Europe. It emphasized that knowledge is an innate possession of reason.

**Rawlsian:** ideas that broadly follow the work of John Rawls.

**Recognition:** an idea central to Hegel's thought, whereby a self-conscious being is unaware that he is self-conscious until he is confronted by another self-conscious being, when he then desires to be recognized as such. This aspect of human nature has many implications for political society and can be applied to widely divergent academic fields.

**Reductionism:** in the philosophy of the mind, the attempt to reduce mental states to nonmental states, such as brain states, functional states, or behavioral states.

**Revolutionary War (1775–83):** (also known as the American War of Independence), a conflict between Britain and the 13 colonies of America that eventually drew in France, Spain, and the Netherlands.

**Russian Revolution:** two revolutions, in March and October 1917, that swept away the autocratic rule of Tsar Nicholas II and introduced communist government, leading eventually to the establishment of the Soviet Union.

**Serfdom:** a system that existed during the European Middle Ages whereby a person was effectively tied to the land. Land would be given by its owner to the serf in return for the serf working the lord's fields, mines, forests, or roads.

*Selbst:* German word meaning personally or "oneself".

**Social contract theory:** the idea that governments are formed when a social group agrees to be ruled by a ruler or ruling class so that their lives and certain fundamental rights can be protected. This implies that governments that do not provide these functions are illegitimate.

**Soviet Union, or USSR:** a kind of "super state" that existed from 1922 to 1991, centered primarily on Russia and its neighbors in Eastern Europe and the northern half of Asia. It was the communist pole of the Cold War, with the United States as its main "rival."

**Standpoint of the consciousness:** refers to Hegel's belief that neither our everyday experience nor the philosophical tradition was capable of properly understanding the relationship between the mind and the world.

**Totalitarianism:** a political system in which the state exercises absolute or near-absolute control over society.

**Transcendental dialectic:** In *Critique of Pure Reason*, Immanuel Kant described the futility in trying to find meaning behind transcendental categories using the senses alone. The transcendental, according to Immanuel Kant, was comprised of all things that lay outside of human experience.

**Transcendental Idealism:** philosophical idea that argues human experience of objects is governed by the senses. According to Kant, our perception of objects is necessarily subjective and we do not necessarily understand them as they are in reality. The transcendental, according to Immanuel Kant, was comprised of all things that lay outside of human experience.

**Triadic structure:** the three-part structure that forms part of the Hegelian dialectic, although it is important to note Hegel himself did not use this term. Its three parts are: thesis—a thought that has proved to be unsatisfactory; antithesis—a negation of the original idea that also proves to be unsatisfactory; and synthesis—a new thought, which is again negated and will continue to be negated as long as the idea proves unsatisfactory.

**Young Hegelianism**: (also known as "left" Hegelianism), this is a philosophical school of thought that developed in the decades immediately following Hegel's death in 1831. Whereas the "right" Hegelians emphasized the religious aspects of Hegel's thought and were politically conservative, the "left" Hegelians were progressive and often revolutionary in temperament and rejected Hegel's idealism in favor of "realism" or materialism.

**World War II**: Global conflict between 1939 and 1945 that pitted the Axis Powers of Nazi Germany, Fascist Italy, and Imperial Japan against the Allied nations including Britain, the United States, and the USSR.

# PEOPLE MENTIONED IN THE TEXT

**Louis Althusser (1918–90)** was a French Marxist philosopher who taught at the École Normale Supérieure in Paris. His works include *The Return to Hegel* (1950) and *For Marx* (1965).

**Aristotle (384–322 B.C.E.)** was a Greek philosopher. Together with his teacher, Plato, he is one of the key originators of Western philosophy. Aristotle wrote and taught on a wide range of topics, from rhetoric and poetry to physics and ethics.

**Raymond Aron (1905–83)** was a French philosopher and sociologist. His 1955 work *The Opium of the Intellectuals* criticized the tolerance of the French intellectual classes for oppressive Marxist regimes. Other works include *Main Currents in Sociological Thought* (1965) and *History and the Dialectic of Violence* (1975).

**Shlomo Avineri (b. 1933)** is an Israeli political scientist. He has written extensively on the history of philosophy, especially that of Marx and Hegel.

**Frederick Beiser (b. 1949)** is a German philosopher best known for his work on German Idealism and German Romanticism. He is currently professor of philosophy at Syracuse University.

**Isaiah Berlin (1909–97)** was a political theorist who not only taught at Oxford University but also helped found Oxford's Wolfson College. His most important work centered on individual freedom and liberty.

**Napoleon Bonaparte (1769–1821)** was a French military and political leader who originated from Corsica. His meteoric rise to power changed the face of Europe forever and instigated a period of almost continuous warfare between 1803 and 1815 that involved every major European power.

**Robert Brandom (b. 1950)** is a distinguished professor and fellow of the American Academy of Arts and Sciences. He currently teaches in the philosophy department of the University of Pittsburgh.

**René Descartes (1596–1650)** was a French mathematician and philosopher. Due to such works as the *Discourse on Method* (1637) and *Meditations on First Philosophy* (1641), he is commonly known as the father of modern philosophy.

**Ludwig Feuerbach (1804–72)** was a German "left-Hegelian" philosopher. He is best known for the critique of religion he outlined in his 1841 *The Essence of Christianity*. Feuerbach claimed that belief in a transcendent deity involved projecting humanity's "species being" onto a fictional entity.

**Johann Gottlieb Fichte (1762–1814)** was the first of the three major philosophers of German Idealism, the others being F. W. J. Schelling and Hegel. Fichte's position continually evolved throughout his philosophical career. He introduced the idea of mutual recognition, which is central to *Phenomenology*.

**Michael Forster (b. 1957)** is a philosopher who teaches at Bonn University in Germany and at the University of Chicago in the United States.

**J. F. Fries (1773–1843)** was a German philosopher and professor at the University of Heidelberg. He was politically active and influential on the politics of student fraternities. He combined nationalism with a form of unionism and liberalism. He also advocated discrimination against Jews and published anti-Semitic propaganda. He was Hegel's chief philosophical and personal enemy.

**Francis Fukuyama (b. 1952)** is an American political philosopher. He is best known for his 1992 work *The End of History and the Last Man*, which drew heavily from Alexandre Kojève's interpretation of Hegel, especially where it concerned the struggle for recognition.

**Hans Friedrich Fulda** is a professor of philosophy at Heidelberg University. His publications include work on Kant, Hegel, and metaphysics.

**Johann Wolfgang von Goethe (1749–1832)** was a German polymath and statesman. Goethe was instrumental in furthering both Hegel's career and his philosophy of science.

**H. S. Harris (1926–2007)** was a British professor of philosophy. An acknowledged authority on the works of Hegel, he taught at York University until his retirement in 1996.

**Martin Heidegger (1889–1976)** was a German philosopher. He wrote in the tradition of phenomenology, but can be said to have founded a school of philosophy in his own right, being one of the most influential philosophers of the twentieth century.

**Johann Gottfried Herder (1744–1803)** was a German poet and philosopher. He was a key figure both of the *Sturm und Drang* ("storm and stress") movement and Weimar Classicism. This literary movement, a reaction to rationalism, allowed for the free expression of extreme emotion.

**Thomas Hobbes (1588–1679)** was an English philosopher. His *Leviathan* of 1651 is a seminal text of modern political thought. Hobbes argued that individuals must exit the warlike "state of nature" and enter into a social contract whereby they submit to an absolute sovereign.

**Axel Honneth (b. 1949)** is a professor of philosophy and currently the director of the Institute for Social Research in Frankfurt. He has written several books on the Hegelian concept of a struggle for recognition.

**Stephen Houlgate (b. 1954)** is a Hegel specialist who has written a number of books on Hegel and his work, including one published in 2013 devoted to *Phenomenology of Spirit*.

**Jean Hyppolite (1907–68)** was a French philosopher who focused much of his life's work on German philosophers, especially Hegel.

**F. H. Jacobi (1743–1819)** was a German merchant, civil servant, novelist, and philosopher.

**William James (1842–1910)** was an American philosopher and psychologist and one of the founders of pragmatist philosophy. His works include *The Principles of Psychology* (1890), *The Varieties of Religious Experience* (1902), and *Essays in Radical Empiricism* (1912).

**Immanuel Kant (1724–1804)** was a German philosopher based in Königsberg, now called Kaliningrad. He is famous for his so-called "critical philosophy," which is principally laid out in his three great "Critiques": the *Critique of Pure Reason* (1781; second edition, 1787), the *Critique of Practical Reason* (1788), and the *Critique of the Power of Judgment* (1790).

**Alexandre Kojève (1902–68)** was a Russian-born French philosopher who is best remembered for his work on Hegel, delivered via a series of lectures. In recent years, his work has been reevaluated by scholars such as Francis Fukuyama.

**Jacques Lacan (1901–81)** was a French psychoanalyst. His theories combined influences from such varied fields as Freudian psychoanalysis, poststructuralist linguistics, and mathematics.

**Gottfried Wilhelm Leibniz (1646–1716)** was a German rationalist philosopher, mathematician, jurist, and polymath. He made numerous contributions to science and mathematics, including his independent discovery of the infinitesimal calculus.

**John Locke (1632–1704)** was an English philosopher who made seminal contributions to empiricist philosophy and political theory. His most celebrated works are *An Essay Concerning Human Understanding* (1689) and *Two Treatises of Government* (1690).

**Alasdair MacIntyre (b. 1929)** is a Scottish philosopher and senior research fellow at London Metropolitan University. His 1981 text, *After Virtue,* is considered to be seminal.

**Karl Marx (1818–83)** was a German economist and philosopher, and the preeminent theorist of communism; his major work is *Das Kapital* (1867–94). The young Marx was a "young Hegelian" thinker.

**John McDowell (b. 1942)** is a South African professor of philosophy who currently works at the University of Pittsburgh. He has written extensively in the fields of epistemology and metaphysics.

**Moses Mendelssohn (1729–86)** was a German Jewish philosopher and stalwart of the Berlin Enlightenment. His thought belonged to the rationalist school of Leibniz and Christian Wolff.

**George Edward Moore (1873–1958)** was an English philosopher who advocated "common sense" in philosophical method and common-sense realism.

**Friedrich Immanuel Niethammer (1766–1848)** was a German theologian and philosopher. A professor of philosophy in Jena until 1804, he became Central Commissioner of Education and a member of the Consistory of Bavaria in 1807. He had met Hegel when a student at Tübingen and frequently assisted the advancement of Hegel's career.

**Novalis** is the pen name of the German aristocrat Friedrich Freiherr von Hardenberg (1772–1801). He was associated with the Romantics in Jena. One of the few works published in his lifetime was his *Hymns to the Night* (1800).

**Terry Pinkard (b. 1953)** is a professor at Georgetown University. He has produced four books on Hegel's work to date.

**Robert Pippin (b. 1948)** is an American philosopher who specializes in Hegel. He holds the post of PhD Honoris Causa at Uppsala University in Sweden.

**Plato (427–347 B.C.E)** was an ancient Greek philosopher. With Socrates and Aristotle, Plato was one of the three great founding thinkers in the Western philosophical tradition.

**Karl Popper (1902–94)** was an Austrian British philosopher whose work *The Open Society and its Enemies* (1945) marked him as one of the most influential scholars of the twentieth century.

**Michael Quante (b. 1962)** is a German philosopher and *Hochschuldozent* (senior lecturer) in the Philosophisches Seminar des Westfalischen Wilhelms-Universität, Münster. He is an acknowledged expert on the works of Hegel.

**John Rawls (1921–2002)** was an American political philosopher. His work *A Theory of Justice* (1971) is one of the most important texts in the whole field of political philosophy.

**K. L. Reinhold (1757–1823)** was a German philosopher. His *Letters on the Kantian Philosophy* (1786–87) brought Kant's critical philosophy to a wider audience at the expense of its nuances.

**Richard Rorty (1931–2007)** was an American philosopher best known for his work in analytic philosophy. He taught at a number of universities during his long career, including Stanford and Princeton.

**Bertrand Russell (1872–1970)** was a British philosopher, logician, and political activist. Together with German philosopher

Gottlob Frege (1848–1925), he was one of the principal founders of the analytic school of philosophy.

**Gilbert Ryle (1900–76)** was a British philosopher interested in linguistics and behaviorism. He is best remembered for his work *The Concept of Mind* (1949).

**Michael Sandel (b. 1953)** is an American philosopher who currently teaches at Harvard University. In his first book, *Liberalism and the Limits of Justice* (1982), he was highly critical of John Rawls.

**Jean-Paul Sartre (1905–80)** was a French writer and novelist. He authored plays, novels, screenplays, and journalistic articles, as well as philosophical treatises. He was France's most prominent postwar public intellectual, and an exponent of existentialist philosophy and Marxism. (Existentialism is a philosophical movement that began in the late nineteenth century; its proponents argued that the origin point of philosophical thought stems from human individuality. They included in this category all aspects of the individual as a thinking, feeling, acting individual.)

**Friedrich Wilhelm Joseph Schelling (1775–1854)** was a German Idealist philosopher. A roommate of Hegel's in the Tübingen seminary, the two collaborated on a common philosophical project. The publication of *Phenomenology*, with its stinging critiques of Schelling, signaled that each would follow his own separate path.

**Friedrich Schiller (1759–1805)** was a German poet, philosopher, and playwright. He is known especially for his plays *The Robbers* (1781) and *William Tell* (1804). His poem "Ode to Joy" became the basis of the famous final choral section of Beethoven's Ninth Symphony.

**Karl Wilhelm Friedrich Schlegel (1772–1829)** was a German poet and critic. He was, with his brother August, a prominent figure of German Romanticism. Hegel was from early on a stern critic of Schlegel's advocacy of Romantic irony.

**Wilfrid Sellars (1912–89)** was an American philosopher who helped develop the school of thought known as Critical Realism. His most famous work remains his Hegelian *Empiricism and the Philosophy of the Mind* (1954).

**Socrates (470/469–399 B.C.E.)** was an ancient Greek philosopher and one of the founding fathers of Western Philosophy. His work is mostly known thanks to its discussion by Plato, since little of his original work survived.

**Benedictus de Spinoza (1632–77)** was a Jewish Dutch philosopher in the rationalist tradition. His main works are *Tractatus Theologico-Politicus* (1673) and *Ethics* (1677). Spinoza's name was synonymous with atheism and fatalism in Europe.

**Gottlob Storr (1746–1805)** was a leading Tübingen theologian. He was an advocate of what is known as Biblical Supernaturalism.

**Peter Strawson (1919–2006)** was an English philosopher who taught at Oxford University for most of his career. He is known for his work in metaphysics.

**Charles Taylor (b. 1931)** is a Canadian philosopher and professor emeritus at McGill University. His work includes a focus on the history of philosophy and the philosophy of social science.

**Thrasymachus (459–400 B.C.E.)** is mentioned in Plato's *Republic*, where he is depicted as a Sophist who entered into a number of disagreements with Socrates.

**Michael Walzer (b. 1935)** is an American political theorist and professor emeritus at Princeton University. He specializes in political ethics.

**Joachim Winkelmann (1717–68)** was a German art historian. His 1764 work, *The History of Ancient Art*, had a profound impact on Hegel and many of his contemporaries.

**Christian Wolff (1679–1754)** was a German philosopher. He wrote on almost every scholarly subject of his time and tried to give systematic and mathematical form to a broadly rationalist and Leibnizian philosophical world-view.

# WORKS CITED

# WORKS CITED

Ameriks, Karl. "The Legacy of Idealism in the Philosophy of Feuerbach, Marx, and Kierkegaard." In *The Cambridge Companion to German Idealism*, edited by Karl Ameriks, 258–82. Cambridge: Cambridge University Press, 2000.

Avineri, Shlomo. *Hegel's Theory of the Modern State*. Cambridge: Cambridge University Press, 1972.

Beiser, Frederick. "Dark Days: Anglophone Scholarship Since the 1960s." In *German Idealism: Contemporary Perspectives*, edited by Espen Hammer, 70–91. Abingdon: Routledge, 2007.

Berlin, Isaiah. *Four Essays on Liberty*. Oxford: Oxford University Press, 1969.

Bonsiepen, Wolfgang. "Erste Zeitgenössische Rezensionen der Phänomenologie des Geistes." *Hegel-Studien* 14 (1979): 9–38.

Brandom, Robert. *Tales of the Mighty Dead: Historical Essays in the Metaphysics of Intentionality*. London: Harvard University Press, 2002.

Engels, Friedrich. Preface to the third (1885) German edition of Karl Marx's *The Eighteenth Brumaire of Louis Bonaparte*. In *Karl Marx and Frederick Engels Selected Works*. Moscow: Progress Publishers, 1968. Accessed August 11, 2015, https://www.marxists.org/archive/marx/works/1885/prefaces/18th-brumaire.htm.

Fanon, Frantz. *Black Skin, White Masks*. Translated by Charles Lam Markmann. London: Pluto Press, 1986.

Forster, Michael N. *Hegel's Idea of a Phenomenology of Spirit*. Chicago: University of Chicago Press, 1998.

Fukuyama, Francis. *The End of History and the Last Man*. London: Penguin, 1992.

Fulda, Hans Friedrich. *Das Problem einer Einleitung in Hegels Wissenschaft der Logik*. Frankfurt am Main: Klostermann, 1965.

Harris, Henry Silton. *Hegel's Ladder*. 2 vols. Cambridge: Hackett, 1997.

Haym, Rudolf. *Hegel und seine Zeit*. Berlin: R. Gaertner, 1857.

Hegel, Georg Wilhelm Friedrich. *The Difference between Fichte's and Schelling's Systems of Philosophy*. Edited by Walter Cerf and H. S. Harris. Albany: State University of New York Press, 1988.

___. *Elements of the Philosophy of Right*. Translated by H. B. Nisbet and edited by Allen Wood. Cambridge: Cambridge University Press, 1991.

\_\_\_\_. *Faith and Knowledge*. Edited by Walter Cerf and H. S. Harris. Albany: State University of New York Press, 1988.

\_\_\_\_. *The Letters*. Translated by Clark Butler and Christiane Seiler. Bloomington: University of Indiana Press, 1984.

\_\_\_\_. "On the Prospects for a Folk Religion." In *Three Essays, 1793–1795,* edited and translated by Peter Fuss and John Dobbins, 30–58. Notre Dame, Indiana: University of Notre Dame Press, 1984.

\_\_\_\_. *Phenomenology of Spirit*. Translated by A. V. Miller. Oxford: Oxford University Press, 1977.

\_\_\_\_. *The Science of Logic*. Translated by George Di Giovanni. Cambridge: Cambridge University Press, 2015.

\_\_\_\_. *The Science of Logic: 1, Encyclopedia of the Philosophical Sciences.* Translated by William Wallace. US: Hythloday Press, 2014.

\_\_\_\_. *System of Ethical Life*. Edited and translated by T. M. Knox. Albany: State University of New York Press, 1979.

Hobbes, Thomas. *Leviathan: Cambridge Texts in the History of Political Thought*. Edited by Richard Tuck. Cambridge; New York: Cambridge University Press, 1991.

Honneth, Axel. *The Struggle for Recognition*. Translated by Joel Anderson. Cambridge: Polity Press, 1995.

Houlgate, Stephen. *Hegel's "Phenomenology of Spirit": A Reader's Guide*. London & New York: Bloomsbury Publishing, 2013.

\_\_\_\_. *The Opening of Hegel's Logic: From Being to Infinity*. West Lafayette, IN: Purdue University Press, 2006.

Hyppolite, Jean. *Genesis and Structure of Hegel's* Phenomenology of Spirit. Translated by Samuel Cherniak and John Heckman. Evanston: Northwestern University Press, 1974.

Kojève, Alexandre. *Introduction to the Reading of Hegel: Lectures on* Phenomenology of Spirit. Translated by James H. Nichols, Jr. New York: Basic Books, 1969.

Kreines, James. "Hegel's Metaphysics: Changing the Debate." *Philosophy Compass* 1.5 (2006): 466–80.

Lukács, George. *The Young Hegel*. Translated by Rodney Livingstone. London: Merlin Press, 1975.

Marx, Karl. *Critique of Hegel's "Philosophy of Right."* Edited by Joseph O'Malley. Cambridge: Cambridge University Press, 1977.

McDowell, John. *Having the World in View: Essays on Kant, Hegel, and Schelling*. London: Harvard University Press, 2009.

Nicolin, Gunther (editor). *Hegel in Berichten seiner Zeitgenossen*. Hamburg: Felix Meiner Verlag, 1970.

Nimbalkar, Namita. "John Locke on Personal Identity." *Mens Sana Monographs*. 9.1 (2011): 268–75.

Pinkard, Terry. *Hegel: A Biography*. Cambridge: Cambridge University Press, 2000.

Pippin, Robert B. *Hegel's Idealism: The Satisfactions of Self-Consciousness*. Cambridge: Cambridge University Press, 1989.

Popper, Karl. *The Open Society and Its Enemies, Vol. 2. The High Tide of Prophecy: Hegel, Marx, and the Aftermath*. London: Routledge, 1952.

Quante, Michael. *Hegel's Concept of Action*. Translated by Dean Moyar. Cambridge: Cambridge University Press, 2004.

Rawls, John. *A Theory of Justice*. Cambridge, MA: Harvard University Press, 1971.

Rorty, Richard. "The Historiography of Philosophy: Four Genres." In *Philosophy in History*, edited by Richard Rorty, J. B. Schneewind, and Quentin Skinner, 31–49. Cambridge: Cambridge University Press, 1984.

Sellars, Wilfrid. "Empiricism and the Philosophy of Mind." In *Minnesota Studies in the Philosophy of Science, Volume I: The Foundations of Science and the Concepts of Psychology and Psychoanalysis*, edited by Herbert Feigl and Michael Scriven, 253–329. Minneapolis: University of Minnesota Press, 1956.

Singer, Peter. *Hegel*. Oxford: Oxford University Press, 1983.

Strawson, Peter. *Bounds of Sense: An Essay on Kant's* Critique of Pure Reason. London: Methuen, 1966.

Taylor, Charles. *Hegel*. Cambridge: Cambridge University Press, 1975.

____. *Sources of the Self: The Making of the Modern Identity.* Cambridge, MA: Harvard University Press, 1989.

Theunissen, Michael. *Hegels Lehre Vom Absoluten Geist Als Theologisch-Politischer Traktat*. Berlin: de Gruyter, 1970.

Ugilt, Rasmus. *The Metaphysics of Terror: The Incoherent System of Contemporary Politics.* London & New York: Bloomsbury Academic, 2012.

# THE MACAT LIBRARY
# BY DISCIPLINE

**AFRICANA STUDIES**

Chinua Achebe's *An Image of Africa: Racism in Conrad's Heart of Darkness*
W. E. B. Du Bois's *The Souls of Black Folk*
Zora Neale Huston's *Characteristics of Negro Expression*
Martin Luther King Jr's *Why We Can't Wait*
Toni Morrison's *Playing in the Dark: Whiteness in the American Literary Imagination*

**ANTHROPOLOGY**

Arjun Appadurai's *Modernity at Large: Cultural Dimensions of Globalisation*
Philippe Ariès's *Centuries of Childhood*
Franz Boas's *Race, Language and Culture*
Kim Chan & Renée Mauborgne's *Blue Ocean Strategy*
Jared Diamond's *Guns, Germs & Steel: the Fate of Human Societies*
Jared Diamond's *Collapse: How Societies Choose to Fail or Survive*
E. E. Evans-Pritchard's *Witchcraft, Oracles and Magic Among the Azande*
James Ferguson's *The Anti-Politics Machine*
Clifford Geertz's *The Interpretation of Cultures*
David Graeber's *Debt: the First 5000 Years*
Karen Ho's *Liquidated: An Ethnography of Wall Street*
Geert Hofstede's *Culture's Consequences: Comparing Values, Behaviors, Institutes and Organizations across Nations*
Claude Lévi-Strauss's *Structural Anthropology*
Jay Macleod's *Ain't No Makin' It: Aspirations and Attainment in a Low-Income Neighborhood*
Saba Mahmood's *The Politics of Piety: The Islamic Revival and the Feminist Subject*
Marcel Mauss's *The Gift*

**BUSINESS**

Jean Lave & Etienne Wenger's *Situated Learning*
Theodore Levitt's *Marketing Myopia*
Burton G. Malkiel's *A Random Walk Down Wall Street*
Douglas McGregor's *The Human Side of Enterprise*
Michael Porter's *Competitive Strategy: Creating and Sustaining Superior Performance*
John Kotter's *Leading Change*
C. K. Prahalad & Gary Hamel's *The Core Competence of the Corporation*

**CRIMINOLOGY**

Michelle Alexander's *The New Jim Crow: Mass Incarceration in the Age of Colorblindness*
Michael R. Gottfredson & Travis Hirschi's *A General Theory of Crime*
Richard Herrnstein & Charles A. Murray's *The Bell Curve: Intelligence and Class Structure in American Life*
Elizabeth Loftus's *Eyewitness Testimony*
Jay Macleod's *Ain't No Makin' It: Aspirations and Attainment in a Low-Income Neighborhood*
Philip Zimbardo's *The Lucifer Effect*

**ECONOMICS**

Janet Abu-Lughod's *Before European Hegemony*
Ha-Joon Chang's *Kicking Away the Ladder*
David Brion Davis's *The Problem of Slavery in the Age of Revolution*
Milton Friedman's *The Role of Monetary Policy*
Milton Friedman's *Capitalism and Freedom*
David Graeber's *Debt: the First 5000 Years*
Friedrich Hayek's *The Road to Serfdom*
Karen Ho's *Liquidated: An Ethnography of Wall Street*

The Macat Library By Discipline

John Maynard Keynes's *The General Theory of Employment, Interest and Money*
Charles P. Kindleberger's *Manias, Panics and Crashes*
Robert Lucas's *Why Doesn't Capital Flow from Rich to Poor Countries?*
Burton G. Malkiel's *A Random Walk Down Wall Street*
Thomas Robert Malthus's *An Essay on the Principle of Population*
Karl Marx's *Capital*
Thomas Piketty's *Capital in the Twenty-First Century*
Amartya Sen's *Development as Freedom*
Adam Smith's *The Wealth of Nations*
Nassim Nicholas Taleb's *The Black Swan: The Impact of the Highly Improbable*
Amos Tversky's & Daniel Kahneman's *Judgment under Uncertainty: Heuristics and Biases*
Mahbub Ul Haq's *Reflections on Human Development*
Max Weber's *The Protestant Ethic and the Spirit of Capitalism*

### FEMINISM AND GENDER STUDIES

Judith Butler's *Gender Trouble*
Simone De Beauvoir's *The Second Sex*
Michel Foucault's *History of Sexuality*
Betty Friedan's *The Feminine Mystique*
Saba Mahmood's *The Politics of Piety: The Islamic Revival and the Feminist Subject*
Joan Wallach Scott's *Gender and the Politics of History*
Mary Wollstonecraft's *A Vindication of the Rights of Woman*
Virginia Woolf's *A Room of One's Own*

### GEOGRAPHY

The Brundtland Report's *Our Common Future*
Rachel Carson's *Silent Spring*
Charles Darwin's *On the Origin of Species*
James Ferguson's *The Anti-Politics Machine*
Jane Jacobs's *The Death and Life of Great American Cities*
James Lovelock's *Gaia: A New Look at Life on Earth*
Amartya Sen's *Development as Freedom*
Mathis Wackernagel & William Rees's *Our Ecological Footprint*

### HISTORY

Janet Abu-Lughod's *Before European Hegemony*
Benedict Anderson's *Imagined Communities*
Bernard Bailyn's *The Ideological Origins of the American Revolution*
Hanna Batatu's *The Old Social Classes And The Revolutionary Movements Of Iraq*
Christopher Browning's *Ordinary Men: Reserve Police Batallion 101 and the Final Solution in Poland*
Edmund Burke's *Reflections on the Revolution in France*
William Cronon's *Nature's Metropolis: Chicago And The Great West*
Alfred W. Crosby's *The Columbian Exchange*
Hamid Dabashi's *Iran: A People Interrupted*
David Brion Davis's *The Problem of Slavery in the Age of Revolution*
Nathalie Zemon Davis's *The Return of Martin Guerre*
Jared Diamond's *Guns, Germs & Steel: the Fate of Human Societies*
Frank Dikotter's *Mao's Great Famine*
John W Dower's *War Without Mercy: Race And Power In The Pacific War*
W. E. B. Du Bois's *The Souls of Black Folk*
Richard J. Evans's *In Defence of History*
Lucien Febvre's *The Problem of Unbelief in the 16th Century*
Sheila Fitzpatrick's *Everyday Stalinism*

Eric Foner's *Reconstruction: America's Unfinished Revolution, 1863-1877*
Michel Foucault's *Discipline and Punish*
Michel Foucault's *History of Sexuality*
Francis Fukuyama's *The End of History and the Last Man*
John Lewis Gaddis's *We Now Know: Rethinking Cold War History*
Ernest Gellner's *Nations and Nationalism*
Eugene Genovese's *Roll, Jordan, Roll: The World the Slaves Made*
Carlo Ginzburg's *The Night Battles*
Daniel Goldhagen's *Hitler's Willing Executioners*
Jack Goldstone's *Revolution and Rebellion in the Early Modern World*
Antonio Gramsci's *The Prison Notebooks*
Alexander Hamilton, John Jay & James Madison's *The Federalist Papers*
Christopher Hill's *The World Turned Upside Down*
Carole Hillenbrand's *The Crusades: Islamic Perspectives*
Thomas Hobbes's *Leviathan*
Eric Hobsbawm's *The Age Of Revolution*
John A. Hobson's *Imperialism: A Study*
Albert Hourani's *History of the Arab Peoples*
Samuel P. Huntington's *The Clash of Civilizations and the Remaking of World Order*
C. L. R. James's *The Black Jacobins*
Tony Judt's *Postwar: A History of Europe Since 1945*
Ernst Kantorowicz's *The King's Two Bodies: A Study in Medieval Political Theology*
Paul Kennedy's *The Rise and Fall of the Great Powers*
Ian Kershaw's *The "Hitler Myth": Image and Reality in the Third Reich*
John Maynard Keynes's *The General Theory of Employment, Interest and Money*
Charles P. Kindleberger's *Manias, Panics and Crashes*
Martin Luther King Jr's *Why We Can't Wait*
Henry Kissinger's *World Order: Reflections on the Character of Nations and the Course of History*
Thomas Kuhn's *The Structure of Scientific Revolutions*
Georges Lefebvre's *The Coming of the French Revolution*
John Locke's *Two Treatises of Government*
Niccolò Machiavelli's *The Prince*
Thomas Robert Malthus's *An Essay on the Principle of Population*
Mahmood Mamdani's *Citizen and Subject: Contemporary Africa And The Legacy Of Late Colonialism*
Karl Marx's *Capital*
Stanley Milgram's *Obedience to Authority*
John Stuart Mill's *On Liberty*
Thomas Paine's *Common Sense*
Thomas Paine's *Rights of Man*
Geoffrey Parker's *Global Crisis: War, Climate Change and Catastrophe in the Seventeenth Century*
Jonathan Riley-Smith's *The First Crusade and the Idea of Crusading*
Jean-Jacques Rousseau's *The Social Contract*
Joan Wallach Scott's *Gender and the Politics of History*
Theda Skocpol's *States and Social Revolutions*
Adam Smith's *The Wealth of Nations*
Timothy Snyder's *Bloodlands: Europe Between Hitler and Stalin*
Sun Tzu's *The Art of War*
Keith Thomas's *Religion and the Decline of Magic*
Thucydides's *The History of the Peloponnesian War*
Frederick Jackson Turner's *The Significance of the Frontier in American History*
Odd Arne Westad's *The Global Cold War: Third World Interventions And The Making Of Our Times*

The Macat Library By Discipline

**LITERATURE**

Chinua Achebe's *An Image of Africa: Racism in Conrad's Heart of Darkness*
Roland Barthes's *Mythologies*
Homi K. Bhabha's *The Location of Culture*
Judith Butler's *Gender Trouble*
Simone De Beauvoir's *The Second Sex*
Ferdinand De Saussure's *Course in General Linguistics*
T. S. Eliot's *The Sacred Wood: Essays on Poetry and Criticism*
Zora Neale Huston's *Characteristics of Negro Expression*
Toni Morrison's *Playing in the Dark: Whiteness in the American Literary Imagination*
Edward Said's *Orientalism*
Gayatri Chakravorty Spivak's *Can the Subaltern Speak?*
Mary Wollstonecraft's *A Vindication of the Rights of Women*
Virginia Woolf's *A Room of One's Own*

**PHILOSOPHY**

Elizabeth Anscombe's *Modern Moral Philosophy*
Hannah Arendt's *The Human Condition*
Aristotle's *Metaphysics*
Aristotle's *Nicomachean Ethics*
Edmund Gettier's *Is Justified True Belief Knowledge?*
Georg Wilhelm Friedrich Hegel's *Phenomenology of Spirit*
David Hume's *Dialogues Concerning Natural Religion*
David Hume's *The Enquiry for Human Understanding*
Immanuel Kant's *Religion within the Boundaries of Mere Reason*
Immanuel Kant's *Critique of Pure Reason*
Søren Kierkegaard's *The Sickness Unto Death*
Søren Kierkegaard's *Fear and Trembling*
C. S. Lewis's *The Abolition of Man*
Alasdair MacIntyre's *After Virtue*
Marcus Aurelius's *Meditations*
Friedrich Nietzsche's *On the Genealogy of Morality*
Friedrich Nietzsche's *Beyond Good and Evil*
Plato's *Republic*
Plato's *Symposium*
Jean-Jacques Rousseau's *The Social Contract*
Gilbert Ryle's *The Concept of Mind*
Baruch Spinoza's *Ethics*
Sun Tzu's *The Art of War*
Ludwig Wittgenstein's *Philosophical Investigations*

**POLITICS**

Benedict Anderson's *Imagined Communities*
Aristotle's *Politics*
Bernard Bailyn's *The Ideological Origins of the American Revolution*
Edmund Burke's *Reflections on the Revolution in France*
John C. Calhoun's *A Disquisition on Government*
Ha-Joon Chang's *Kicking Away the Ladder*
Hamid Dabashi's *Iran: A People Interrupted*
Hamid Dabashi's *Theology of Discontent: The Ideological Foundation of the Islamic Revolution in Iran*
Robert Dahl's *Democracy and its Critics*
Robert Dahl's *Who Governs?*
David Brion Davis's *The Problem of Slavery in the Age of Revolution*

Alexis De Tocqueville's *Democracy in America*
James Ferguson's *The Anti-Politics Machine*
Frank Dikotter's *Mao's Great Famine*
Sheila Fitzpatrick's *Everyday Stalinism*
Eric Foner's *Reconstruction: America's Unfinished Revolution, 1863-1877*
Milton Friedman's *Capitalism and Freedom*
Francis Fukuyama's *The End of History and the Last Man*
John Lewis Gaddis's *We Now Know: Rethinking Cold War History*
Ernest Gellner's *Nations and Nationalism*
David Graeber's *Debt: the First 5000 Years*
Antonio Gramsci's *The Prison Notebooks*
Alexander Hamilton, John Jay & James Madison's *The Federalist Papers*
Friedrich Hayek's *The Road to Serfdom*
Christopher Hill's *The World Turned Upside Down*
Thomas Hobbes's *Leviathan*
John A. Hobson's *Imperialism: A Study*
Samuel P. Huntington's *The Clash of Civilizations and the Remaking of World Order*
Tony Judt's *Postwar: A History of Europe Since 1945*
David C. Kang's *China Rising: Peace, Power and Order in East Asia*
Paul Kennedy's *The Rise and Fall of Great Powers*
Robert Keohane's *After Hegemony*
Martin Luther King Jr.'s *Why We Can't Wait*
Henry Kissinger's *World Order: Reflections on the Character of Nations and the Course of History*
John Locke's *Two Treatises of Government*
Niccolò Machiavelli's *The Prince*
Thomas Robert Malthus's *An Essay on the Principle of Population*
Mahmood Mamdani's *Citizen and Subject: Contemporary Africa And The Legacy Of Late Colonialism*
Karl Marx's *Capital*
John Stuart Mill's *On Liberty*
John Stuart Mill's *Utilitarianism*
Hans Morgenthau's *Politics Among Nations*
Thomas Paine's *Common Sense*
Thomas Paine's *Rights of Man*
Thomas Piketty's *Capital in the Twenty-First Century*
Robert D. Putman's *Bowling Alone*
John Rawls's *Theory of Justice*
Jean-Jacques Rousseau's *The Social Contract*
Theda Skocpol's *States and Social Revolutions*
Adam Smith's *The Wealth of Nations*
Sun Tzu's *The Art of War*
Henry David Thoreau's *Civil Disobedience*
Thucydides's *The History of the Peloponnesian War*
Kenneth Waltz's *Theory of International Politics*
Max Weber's *Politics as a Vocation*
Odd Arne Westad's *The Global Cold War: Third World Interventions And The Making Of Our Times*

**POSTCOLONIAL STUDIES**

Roland Barthes's *Mythologies*
Frantz Fanon's *Black Skin, White Masks*
Homi K. Bhabha's *The Location of Culture*
Gustavo Gutiérrez's *A Theology of Liberation*
Edward Said's *Orientalism*
Gayatri Chakravorty Spivak's *Can the Subaltern Speak?*

The Macat Library By Discipline

**PSYCHOLOGY**

Gordon Allport's *The Nature of Prejudice*
Alan Baddeley & Graham Hitch's *Aggression: A Social Learning Analysis*
Albert Bandura's *Aggression: A Social Learning Analysis*
Leon Festinger's *A Theory of Cognitive Dissonance*
Sigmund Freud's *The Interpretation of Dreams*
Betty Friedan's *The Feminine Mystique*
Michael R. Gottfredson & Travis Hirschi's *A General Theory of Crime*
Eric Hoffer's *The True Believer: Thoughts on the Nature of Mass Movements*
William James's *Principles of Psychology*
Elizabeth Loftus's *Eyewitness Testimony*
A. H. Maslow's *A Theory of Human Motivation*
Stanley Milgram's *Obedience to Authority*
Steven Pinker's *The Better Angels of Our Nature*
Oliver Sacks's *The Man Who Mistook His Wife For a Hat*
Richard Thaler & Cass Sunstein's *Nudge: Improving Decisions About Health, Wealth and Happiness*
Amos Tversky's *Judgment under Uncertainty: Heuristics and Biases*
Philip Zimbardo's *The Lucifer Effect*

**SCIENCE**

Rachel Carson's *Silent Spring*
William Cronon's *Nature's Metropolis: Chicago And The Great West*
Alfred W. Crosby's *The Columbian Exchange*
Charles Darwin's *On the Origin of Species*
Richard Dawkin's *The Selfish Gene*
Thomas Kuhn's *The Structure of Scientific Revolutions*
Geoffrey Parker's *Global Crisis: War, Climate Change and Catastrophe in the Seventeenth Century*
Mathis Wackernagel & William Rees's *Our Ecological Footprint*

**SOCIOLOGY**

Michelle Alexander's *The New Jim Crow: Mass Incarceration in the Age of Colorblindness*
Gordon Allport's *The Nature of Prejudice*
Albert Bandura's *Aggression: A Social Learning Analysis*
Hanna Batatu's *The Old Social Classes And The Revolutionary Movements Of Iraq*
Ha-Joon Chang's *Kicking Away the Ladder*
W. E. B. Du Bois's *The Souls of Black Folk*
Émile Durkheim's *On Suicide*
Frantz Fanon's *Black Skin, White Masks*
Frantz Fanon's *The Wretched of the Earth*
Eric Foner's *Reconstruction: America's Unfinished Revolution, 1863-1877*
Eugene Genovese's *Roll, Jordan, Roll: The World the Slaves Made*
Jack Goldstone's *Revolution and Rebellion in the Early Modern World*
Antonio Gramsci's *The Prison Notebooks*
Richard Herrnstein & Charles A Murray's *The Bell Curve: Intelligence and Class Structure in American Life*
Eric Hoffer's *The True Believer: Thoughts on the Nature of Mass Movements*
Jane Jacobs's *The Death and Life of Great American Cities*
Robert Lucas's *Why Doesn't Capital Flow from Rich to Poor Countries?*
Jay Macleod's *Ain't No Makin' It: Aspirations and Attainment in a Low Income Neighborhood*
Elaine May's *Homeward Bound: American Families in the Cold War Era*
Douglas McGregor's *The Human Side of Enterprise*
C. Wright Mills's *The Sociological Imagination*

Thomas Piketty's *Capital in the Twenty-First Century*
Robert D. Putman's *Bowling Alone*
David Riesman's *The Lonely Crowd: A Study of the Changing American Character*
Edward Said's *Orientalism*
Joan Wallach Scott's *Gender and the Politics of History*
Theda Skocpol's *States and Social Revolutions*
Max Weber's *The Protestant Ethic and the Spirit of Capitalism*

## THEOLOGY

Augustine's *Confessions*
Benedict's *Rule of St Benedict*
Gustavo Gutiérrez's *A Theology of Liberation*
Carole Hillenbrand's *The Crusades: Islamic Perspectives*
David Hume's *Dialogues Concerning Natural Religion*
Immanuel Kant's *Religion within the Boundaries of Mere Reason*
Ernst Kantorowicz's *The King's Two Bodies: A Study in Medieval Political Theology*
Søren Kierkegaard's *The Sickness Unto Death*
C. S. Lewis's *The Abolition of Man*
Saba Mahmood's *The Politics of Piety: The Islamic Revival and the Feminist Subjec*t
Baruch Spinoza's *Ethics*
Keith Thomas's *Religion and the Decline of Magic*

## COMING SOON

Chris Argyris's *The Individual and the Organisation*
Seyla Benhabib's *The Rights of Others*
Walter Benjamin's *The Work Of Art in the Age of Mechanical Reproduction*
John Berger's *Ways of Seeing*
Pierre Bourdieu's *Outline of a Theory of Practice*
Mary Douglas's *Purity and Danger*
Roland Dworkin's *Taking Rights Seriously*
James G. March's *Exploration and Exploitation in Organisational Learning*
Ikujiro Nonaka's *A Dynamic Theory of Organizational Knowledge Creation*
Griselda Pollock's *Vision and Difference*
Amartya Sen's *Inequality Re-Examined*
Susan Sontag's *On Photography*
Yasser Tabbaa's *The Transformation of Islamic Art*
Ludwig von Mises's *Theory of Money and Credit*

# Macat Disciplines

*Access the greatest ideas and thinkers across entire disciplines, including*

## INEQUALITY

**Ha-Joon Chang's,** *Kicking Away the Ladder*

**David Graeber's,** *Debt: The First 5000 Years*

**Robert E. Lucas's,** *Why Doesn't Capital Flow from Rich To Poor Countries?*

**Thomas Piketty's,** *Capital in the Twenty-First Century*

**Amartya Sen's,** *Inequality Re-Examined*

**Mahbub Ul Haq's,** *Reflections on Human Development*

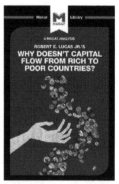

Macat analyses are available from all good bookshops and libraries.

Access hundreds of analyses through one, multimedia tool.

Join free for one month **library.macat.com**

# Macat Disciplines

*Access the greatest ideas and thinkers across entire disciplines, including*

## CRIMINOLOGY

**Michelle Alexander's**
*The New Jim Crow: Mass Incarceration in the Age of Colorblindness*

**Michael R. Gottfredson & Travis Hirschi's**
*A General Theory of Crime*

**Elizabeth Loftus's**
*Eyewitness Testimony*

**Richard Herrnstein & Charles A. Murray's**
*The Bell Curve: Intelligence and Class Structure in American Life*

**Jay Macleod's**
*Ain't No Makin' It: Aspirations and Attainment in a Low-Income Neighborhood*

**Philip Zimbardo's**
*The Lucifer Effect*

Macat analyses are available from all good bookshops and libraries.

Access hundreds of analyses through one, multimedia tool.
Join free for one month **library.macat.com**

# Macat Disciplines

*Access the greatest ideas and thinkers across entire disciplines, including*

## GLOBALIZATION

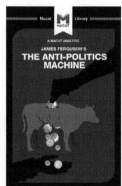

**Arjun Appadurai's,** *Modernity at Large: Cultural Dimensions of Globalisation*

**James Ferguson's,** *The Anti-Politics Machine*

**Geert Hofstede's,** *Culture's Consequences*

**Amartya Sen's,** *Development as Freedom*

Macat analyses are available from all good bookshops and libraries.

Access hundreds of analyses through one, multimedia tool.
Join free for one month **library.macat.com**

# Macat Disciplines

*Access the greatest ideas and thinkers across entire disciplines, including*

## MAN AND THE ENVIRONMENT

**The Brundtland Report's,** *Our Common Future*
**Rachel Carson's,** *Silent Spring*
**James Lovelock's,** *Gaia: A New Look at Life on Earth*
**Mathis Wackernagel & William Rees's,** *Our Ecological Footprint*

Macat analyses are available from all good bookshops and libraries.

Access hundreds of analyses through one, multimedia tool.
Join free for one month **library.macat.com**

Printed in the United States
by Baker & Taylor Publisher Services